Alfred's Great Music & Musicians

An Overview of Keyboard Composers and Literature

Nancy Bachus • Tom Gerou
Edited by Albert Mendoza

A Note to Teachers

The *Great Music & Musicians* series provides a foundation for understanding the major cultural periods, musical styles, and development of music through the ages. The books include art and listening examples to deepen understanding. Although not correlated page by page, Book 2 is appropriate for piano students in various levels of *Premier Piano Course* (based on the individual student's reading level). It also may be used with other piano methods and in group lessons.

The nine units in Book 2 provide overviews of major keyboard composers and literature, as well as information about the development of the piano and related cultural trends. Each unit ends with a short summary and a review activity. At the end of each unit is a *Listening Guide* that includes important keyboard compositions to reinforce the concepts presented. Recordings of these pieces are available online at **alfred.com/GreatMusic2**. Additional listening examples, many of which can be accessed on the Internet, are also suggested. Page 55 contains short biographies of famous pianists from the 19th, 20th, and 21st centuries. An **answer key** for the review activities is provided on page 56. It can be used to quickly check answers after completion of each review activity.

ISBN-10: 0-7390-8761-4
ISBN-13: 978-0-7390-8761-9

Cover art: Franz Liszt Fantasizing at the Piano *(1840)*
by Josef Danhauser (1805–1845)

A Note to Students

*G*reat Music & Musicians, Book 2 will take you on a musical journey throughout history. You will learn how the piano developed and the way this influenced composers and the music they wrote. As you travel through time, you will see important works of art and hear outstanding pieces of keyboard music. You will be able to apply what you learn about keyboard composers and literature to music that you are studying and performing. Enjoy your travels!

Contents

Produced by
Alfred Music
P.O. Box 10003
Van Nuys, CA 91410-0003
alfred.com

Premier Piano Course

Unit 1

Early Keyboards and Composers

Organs

The **hydraulis** was the earliest keyboard instrument and developed in ancient Greece. It was a type of pipe organ in which water pressure forced air into pipes of different lengths and sizes. Levers or keys controlled the wind supply. Eventually, bellows replaced the water device to send air into the pipes. Pipe organs have been in continual use ever since. During the Middle Ages, small **portative organs** were carried in processions or played in intimate settings. Larger **positive organs** were permanently installed in churches. As organs grew in size, three keyboards (called **manuals**) became common. A **pedal keyboard**, played with the feet, controlled the bass pipes.

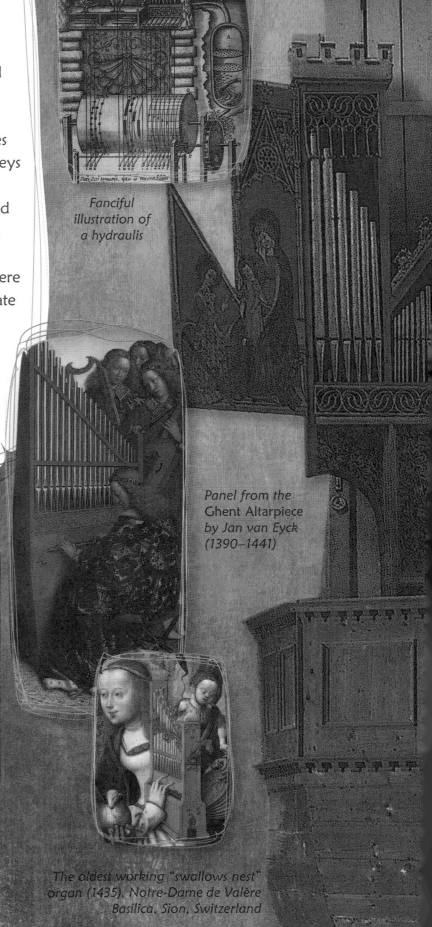

Fanciful illustration of a hydraulis

Panel from the Ghent Altarpiece by Jan van Eyck (1390–1441)

positive organ

portative organ

The oldest working "swallows nest" organ (1435), Notre-Dame de Valère Basilica, Sion, Switzerland

Clavichords and Harpsichords

The first keyboard instrument that used strings to produce sound can be traced to 1360. By the beginning of the Renaissance period in the 1400s, both **clavichords** and **harpsichords** were in existence. Clavichords were often used in homes and played by young women. Known as the "poor man's instrument," the clavichord operated using a simple, metal T-shaped blade on the end of each key, called a **tangent**. Moving the keys created vibrating sounds. Church organists often practiced on clavichords.

Musicians eventually wanted a keyboard instrument that was louder than the clavichord. Harpsichords had strings plucked by small **quills** (made from feathers). Large harpsichords were built with two or three keyboards, controlling three or four sets of strings with varied tone quality and pitches. The different strings and keyboards could be sounded separately or together. Performers made these adjustments with controls called **hand stops** or **coupling levers**. Because of the plucking mechanism, hand pressure had no effect on the instrument's volume. Harpsichords were used for palace concerts, as a part of instrumental ensembles, to accompany vocalists, and as a solo instrument. It was the most popular keyboard instrument until around 1800.

Early harpsichord notation

Tiento del primer tono.

English Virginal Music

English composers in the 16th century were the first to develop a distinct style for playing the harpsichord, known in England as the **virginal**. They composed music well suited for the instrument, often including fast scales and broken chords that fit easily under the hands. Queen Elizabeth I (1533–1603) played the harpsichord and employed many musicians at her court, including composer **William Byrd** (ca. 1540–1623). Byrd's keyboard works are considered among the greatest of the time. *My Ladye Neville's Book* is a famous collection of 42 keyboard pieces by Byrd, probably written for one of his students.

Byrd

Gibbons

Bull

Page from the Fitzwilliam Virginal Book

The Great Hall of Westminster Abbey

Books for the Virginal

The first published keyboard collection, *Parthenia*, was published in London in 16[...] It has 21 pieces by **William Byrd**, **Orlan[...] Gibbons** (1583–1625), and **John Bull** (1562–1628).

Another important keyboard collection from the late Renaissance is *The Fitzwillia[...] Virginal Book*. It contains 297 pieces by various composers. Included are variatio[...] and dances, such as the slow, dignified **pavane** and the fast **galliard**.

Italian Keyboard Composers

The Republic of Venice in northern Italy was an important commercial center and tourist destination in the late Renaissance. It was famous for its canals, opera houses, and carnivals. The renowned music at St. Mark's Basilica in Venice attracted many musicians. They came to study with the cathedral's resident composer, organist, and teacher **Andrea Gabrieli** (ca. 1532–1585). His nephew **Giovanni Gabrieli** (ca. 1557–1612) and student **Claudio Merulo** (1533–1604) followed as organists at St. Mark's. These three composers are best known for their impressive organ works and for developing the **concertato** style—a style with instrumentalists and choirs performing in alternation and together from two separate choir lofts. Keyboard works from this period include elaborate scale passages and are some of the first works to include dynamics. Merulo's **toccatas** (virtuoso keyboard pieces) alternated imitative sections with free, florid sections.

An illustration of concertato style
(with two choir lofts)

Giovanni
Gabrieli (1594)
by Annibale Carracci
(1560–1609)

Merulo

...eyboard piece called a
...nzona" by Frescobaldi

...rolamo **Frescobaldi** (1583–1643)
...mposed pieces in a dramatic
...le. He focused primarily on
...iting keyboard works and was
...e of the first composers to notate
...anges of tempo. He influenced
...ny important composers of the
...oque period.

Piazza San Marco,
Venice, Italy (ca. 1709)
by Luca Carlevarijs
(1663–1730), showing
St. Mark's Basilica

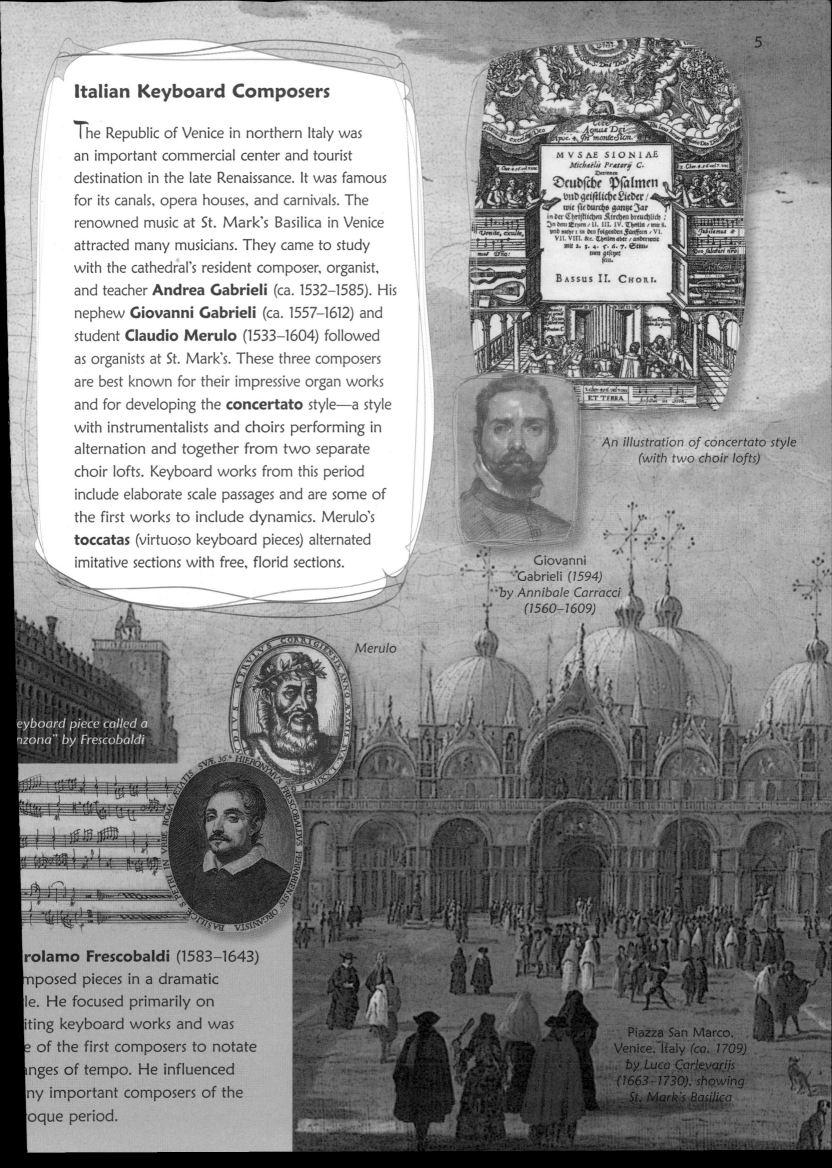

Summary: Early Keyboards and Composers

- Early keyboard instruments included *organs*, *clavichords*, and *harpsichords*.

- In England during the Renaissance period, the harpsichord was known as the *virginal*. The first published keyboard music was *Parthenia*.

- Early Italian composers wrote influential organ works.

- Concertato style involves instrumentalists and choirs performing in alternation and together from two separate choir lofts.

Listening Guide

🔊 Track 1: Toccata del secondo tono
by Giovanni Gabrieli (organ work)

This toccata begins with a few chords, followed by scale passages up and down the keyboard.

🔊 Track 2: Will Yow Walke the Woods soe Wylde
from My Ladye Neville's Book
by William Byrd (virginal work)

This popular song was believed to be a favorite of King Henry VIII. The melody is found in several compositions from the period.

Additional Listening: "Pavan and Galliard of My Lord Lumley" *from* The Fitzwilliam Virginal Book *by John Bull* • Toccata quarta del sesto tono *by Claudio Merulo* • "The Woods so Wilde" *from* The Fitzwilliam Virginal Book *by Orlando Gibbons*

Matching

Match each term with its definition by writing the correct letters on the blank lines.

1. ___ portative organ

2. ___ positive organ

3. ___ manuals

4. ___ toccatas

5. ___ tangent

6. ___ clavichord

7. ___ quill

A. T-shaped blade on the end of clavichord keys

B. small organ that can be carried

C. keyboards

D. plucking mechanism on a harpsichord

E. large, permanently installed organ

F. instrument with a soft, muted sound, usually found in homes

G. virtuoso keyboard pieces with contrasting sections

Unit 2

Baroque Keyboard Composers

Heinrich Schütz (German, 1585–1672) was an organist and an influential composer of his time. After studying in Venice, Italy, with Giovanni Gabrieli, Schütz returned to Germany and combined the Italian style (alternating choirs and instrumentalists) with somber German traditions.

Dieterich Buxtehude (Danish, ca. 1637–1707) is known primarily for his organ works and evening concerts of organ and vocal music. His 19 **preludes and toccatas** form the core of his works.

Due to his popular *Canon in D*, **Johann Pachelbel** (German, 1653–1706) is well known today. In his lifetime, he was a prominent teacher, composer, and organist.

Schütz

Buxtehude

Pachelbel

One of the most famous composers of his time, **Georg Philipp Telemann** (German, 1681–1767) wrote over 4,000 compositions. Although he had no formal training, he could play several instruments and had even composed an opera by the age of 12. At the end of his life, he was employed by the city of Hamburg, the most prestigious music position in Germany. His best-known keyboard works are his **Fantasias** (pieces without a set form).

A Baroque-style organ at Weingarten Abbey, Ravensburg near Baden-Württemberg, Germany.

George Frideric Handel

George Frideric Handel (1685–1759) traveled internationally and won great renown throughout Europe. Born in Germany, he lived 50 years in London. Handel composed instrumental solo works, ensemble music, and operas. His famous *Messiah* is an **oratorio**, a large-scale piece for singers and orchestra. Handel often performed on the organ or harpsichord during intermissions of his operas and oratorios, and he was famous for his improvisations. In a keyboard "duel" with Domenico Scarlatti, Handel was named the winning organist. His best-known keyboard work today is a theme and variations known as the "Harmonious Blacksmith."

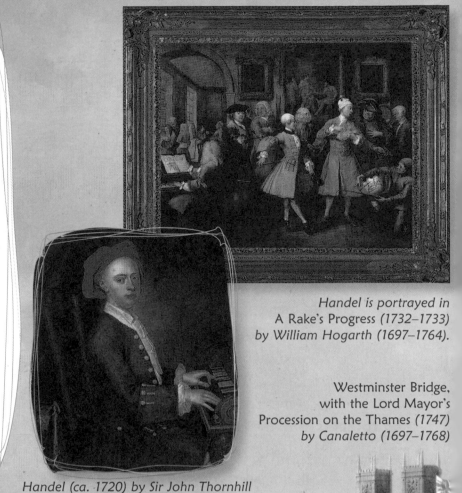

Handel is portrayed in A Rake's Progress *(1732–1733) by William Hogarth (1697–1764).*

Westminster Bridge, with the Lord Mayor's Procession on the Thames (1747) by Canaletto (1697–1768)

Handel (ca. 1720) by Sir John Thornhill (1675–1734)

Domenico Scarlatti (Italian, 1685–1757) spent most of his life at the court in Madrid, Spain. There, he was music master for Queen Maria Barbara (1711–1758). Many of his over 500 keyboard **sonatas** (instrumental pieces) were composed for her. Their repeated notes, cross-hand playing, arpeggios, fast scales, and wide leaps influenced later keyboard works and keyboard playing. Scarlatti's works are identified by the **Kirkpatrick** (**K.** or **Kk.**) catalogue numbers by Ralph Kirkpatrick (American, 1911–1984).

French Clavecin Music

From a family of French musicians, **François Couperin** (1668–1733) was an organist, composer, and teacher at the courts of Louis XIV (1638–1715) and Louis XV (1710–1774). Influenced by English virginalists and French lute music, he composed 27 collections of **clavecin** (French harpsichord) music. These pieces were examples of the newer **galant style** (having charm, elegance, and good taste). Couperin's book *The Art of Playing the Harpsichord* (1716) provides instruction on fingerings and ornaments.

Another French-court composer, **Jean-Philippe Rameau** (1683–1764), also composed keyboard works in galant style, but with greater emotion and technical brilliance.

Couperin

Rameau

Élizabeth-Claude Jacquet de la Guerre *(ca. 1665–1729) lived at the Court of Louis XIV, and she often performed and composed for the King.*

spective view of the Chateau, Gardens,
Park of Versailles (1668) by Pierre Patel
05–1676)

Johann Sebastian Bach

Known as one of the greatest composers of all time, **Johann Sebastian Bach** (German, 1685–1750) combined a variety of styles: German **polyphony** (many voices), French dances, and Italian concertos and sonatas. His compositions are seen as the high point of the Baroque period.

Bach was first taught by his father in Eisenach, Germany. Orphaned at age 10, he went to live with his older brother Johann Christoph, a pupil of Pachelbel. As a choirboy, young Bach learned about French dances, music, and customs.

Bach's first official position was as a church organist. He then composed and directed music for German courts in Weimar and Cöthen. For his last 27 years, Bach was employed by the city of Leipzig. His many responsibilities included providing music for city events, four churches, and festivals at the university. He also trained the choirboys and other students at the St. Thomas School.

Newly discovered portrait of J. S. Bach mentioned in letters of his son C. P. E. Bach

Background: Engraving of Weimar, Germany, where Bach was court organist and began composing The Well-Tempered Clavier

Bach's explanation of ornaments written in his own hand

A double manual harpsichord

Baroque Keyboard Instruments

The organ, harpsichord, and clavichord continued to be played into the Baroque Period (1600–1750). Harpsichord and clavichord keyboards had grown to four and a half octaves. Organ keyboards had less range since the pedal keyboard could play lower notes.

Dance Suites and Concertos

Baroque instrumental music was often inspired by court dances, with pieces frequently grouped into **suites**. Within each suite, the dances shared the same key but were different in tempo, meter, and character. Most keyboard suites included specific dances: **allemande**, **courante**, **sarabande**, and **gigue**. One or more optional dances (**minuet**, **gavotte**, and **polonaise**) could also be included. Bach's *French Suites*, *English Suites*, and *Partitas* follow this pattern.

Bach also wrote suites for solo violin, for solo cello, and for orchestra. His *Brandenburg Concertos* are written for orchestra with various solo instruments. His concertos for harpsichord (one, two, three, or four harpsichord soloists with orchestra) are the first concertos for solo keyboard(s).

Background: St. Thomas School, Leipzig, Germany, where Bach taught for many years

Manuscript from The Well-Tempered Clavier

Georg Fried. Haendel geboren, Joh. Sebast Bach geboren, Joseph Tartini geboren. Joh. Joach. Quanz geboren, Christof Gluck geboren, Nicolo Jomelli geboren.

seven years, Bach directed a **Collegium Musicum** group of amateur
*icians that met at a coffee house. They performed many of his **secular**
(nreligious) works. His harpsichord concertos were written for them.

The Well-Tempered Clavier and the *Inventions and Sinfonias*

Bach composed two collections titled *The Well-Tempered Clavier*. Each collection contains **preludes** (short introductory works) paired with **fugues** (pieces with independent voices). In each book of *The Well-Tempered Clavier*, there is a prelude and a fugue written for every major and minor key.

Bach also wrote 15 *Inventions* and 15 *Sinfonias* as teaching material for his students. At the beginning of the *Inventions*, Bach stated the purpose of these pieces: "to learn to play cleanly in two parts...then proceed...to three...to compose...to achieve a 'singing' style... and to acquire a taste for the elements of composition." Bach's works are identified by the **Bach-Werke-Verzeichnis (BWV)** catalogue numbers by Wolfgang Schmieder (German, 1901–1990).

Summary: Baroque Keyboard Composers

- Italian, French, English, and German composers of the Baroque period developed their own distinct styles, but they also influenced each other.

- *Johann Sebastian Bach* was an important Baroque keyboard composer and virtuoso organist who held different positions in Germany.

- Italian composer *Domenico Scarlatti* wrote many brilliant keyboard sonatas.

- *François Couperin* and *Jean-Philippe Rameau* were two important French composers from the Baroque period, who wrote keyboard music in galant style.

Listening Guide

🔊))) Track 3: "Gigue" *from* French Suite in G Major, BWV 816
by Johann Sebastian Bach
(Baroque dance suite)

This final dance of the suite is in the unusual meter of $\frac{12}{16}$ but feels like it has four beats per measure. Listen for the recurring main theme as it is imitated in the different voices.

🔊))) Track 4: Sonata in D Minor ("Pastorale"), K. 9
by Domenico Scarlatti
(Baroque keyboard sonata)

This sonata has ornaments, scales, and wide leaps. It has two sections, each repeated.

Additional Listening: "Air and Variations" *from* Suite No. 5 in E major ("The Harmonious Blacksmith") *by George Frideric Handel* • Invention No. 8 in F Major, BWV 779, *by Johann Sebastian Bach* • Prelude and Fugue No. 2 in C Minor, BWV 847, *from* The Well-Tempered Clavier, Book 1, *by Johann Sebastian Bach*

Word Search

Find the words and circle them.

B	P	S	C	H	Ü	T	Z	R	H
S	U	A	P	O	D	S	K	A	A
C	C	X	C	F	Ü	J	Y	M	N
O	Y	A	T	H	N	D	I	E	D
U	C	P	R	E	E	I	E	A	E
P	B	D	J	L	H	L	X	U	L
E	N	A	F	N	A	U	B	D	X
R	G	S	C	M	N	T	D	E	H
I	X	A	R	H	T	Ü	T	E	L
N	F	O	L	L	X	O	B	I	G

BACH

BUXTEHUDE

COUPERIN

HANDEL

PACHELBEL

RAMEAU

SCARLATTI

SCHÜTZ

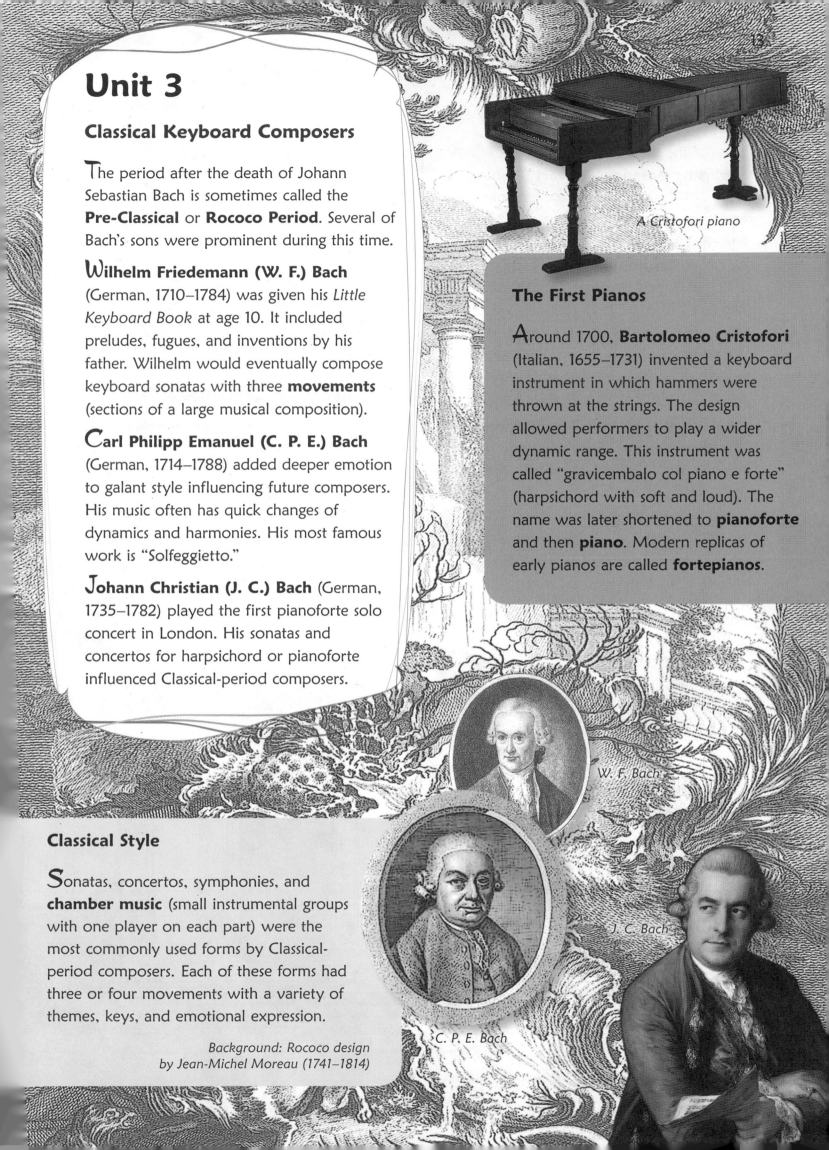

Unit 3

Classical Keyboard Composers

The period after the death of Johann Sebastian Bach is sometimes called the **Pre-Classical** or **Rococo Period**. Several of Bach's sons were prominent during this time.

Wilhelm Friedemann (W. F.) Bach (German, 1710–1784) was given his *Little Keyboard Book* at age 10. It included preludes, fugues, and inventions by his father. Wilhelm would eventually compose keyboard sonatas with three **movements** (sections of a large musical composition).

Carl Philipp Emanuel (C. P. E.) Bach (German, 1714–1788) added deeper emotion to galant style influencing future composers. His music often has quick changes of dynamics and harmonies. His most famous work is "Solfeggietto."

Johann Christian (J. C.) Bach (German, 1735–1782) played the first pianoforte solo concert in London. His sonatas and concertos for harpsichord or pianoforte influenced Classical-period composers.

A Cristofori piano

The First Pianos

Around 1700, **Bartolomeo Cristofori** (Italian, 1655–1731) invented a keyboard instrument in which hammers were thrown at the strings. The design allowed performers to play a wider dynamic range. This instrument was called "gravicembalo col piano e forte" (harpsichord with soft and loud). The name was later shortened to **pianoforte** and then **piano**. Modern replicas of early pianos are called **fortepianos**.

W. F. Bach

Classical Style

Sonatas, concertos, symphonies, and **chamber music** (small instrumental groups with one player on each part) were the most commonly used forms by Classical-period composers. Each of these forms had three or four movements with a variety of themes, keys, and emotional expression.

Background: Rococo design by Jean-Michel Moreau (1741–1814)

C. P. E. Bach

J. C. Bach

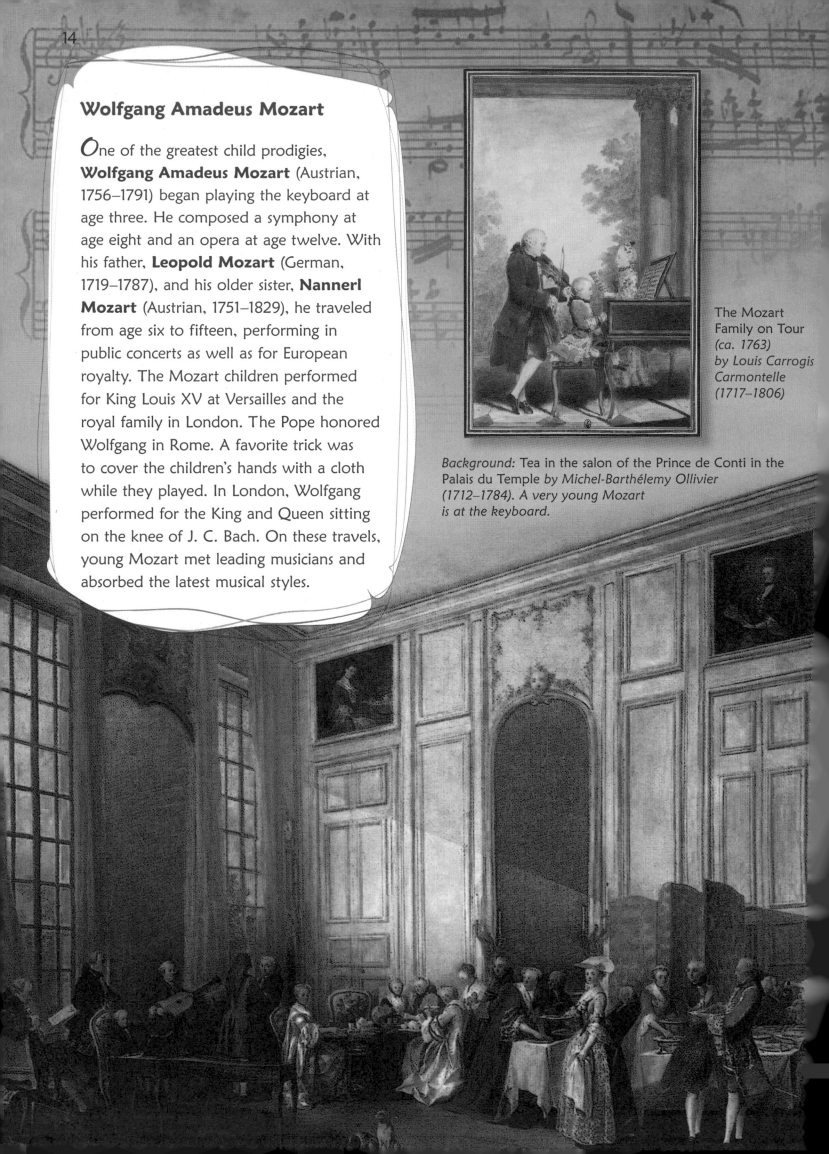

Wolfgang Amadeus Mozart

One of the greatest child prodigies, **Wolfgang Amadeus Mozart** (Austrian, 1756–1791) began playing the keyboard at age three. He composed a symphony at age eight and an opera at age twelve. With his father, **Leopold Mozart** (German, 1719–1787), and his older sister, **Nannerl Mozart** (Austrian, 1751–1829), he traveled from age six to fifteen, performing in public concerts as well as for European royalty. The Mozart children performed for King Louis XV at Versailles and the royal family in London. The Pope honored Wolfgang in Rome. A favorite trick was to cover the children's hands with a cloth while they played. In London, Wolfgang performed for the King and Queen sitting on the knee of J. C. Bach. On these travels, young Mozart met leading musicians and absorbed the latest musical styles.

The Mozart Family on Tour *(ca. 1763) by Louis Carrogis Carmontelle (1717–1806)*

Background: Tea in the salon of the Prince de Conti in the Palais du Temple *by Michel-Barthélemy Ollivier (1712–1784). A very young Mozart is at the keyboard.*

Mozart's Works for Piano

Mozart's solo keyboard works include sonatas, variations, and fantasias. One of his most popular works is the "Rondo Alla Turca" from his *Sonata*, K. 331. He also composed *12 Variations on "Ah, vous dirai-je, maman,"* K. 265 (known by many as the "Twinkle, Twinkle, Little Star" variations).

In his early 20s, Mozart transitioned from performing on harpsichords to pianos. He especially liked those built by Johann Andreas Stein (German, 1728–1792) and Anton Walter (German, 1752–1826). Inspired by these instruments, he composed and performed piano concertos and improvised the **cadenzas** (free sections that show off the technical skills of the soloist). These works elevated the solo piano concerto to new heights.

Mozart Portrait (1789) by Dora Stock (1759–1832)

In his final years, Mozart was always short of money. He borrowed from friends and rented out his home. When the Emperor awarded him a small salary to compose dances for court balls, he said it was "too much for what I do, but too little for what I could do!" Although ill in his final months, he completed the opera *The Magic Flute* and nearly completed a *Requiem Mass* (a Mass for the dead). He died in poverty and was buried in an unmarked grave.

Stage design for Mozart's opera The Magic Flute, K. 620 by Karl Friedrich Schinkel (1781–1841)

Portrait of a young Mozart by Empress Maria Theresa's court painter Martin van Meytens (1695–1770)

Other Works

Mozart's symphonies, piano concertos, and operas are considered to be some of the greatest works of his more than 600 compositions. He transformed opera by adding more serious sections to emphasize each character's humanity, making the dramatic impact of the stories greater. The melodies in his operas are singable, memorable, and popular with the public to this day.

Mozart's works are identified by the **Köchel (K.)** catalogue numbers by Ludwig Ritter von Köchel (Austrian, 1800–1877).

Franz Joseph Haydn

At age five, **Franz Joseph Haydn** (Austrian, 1732–1809) left home to become a choirboy. When his voice changed, he was dismissed from the choir school. As a young man in Vienna, he had difficulty earning a living, but he was eventually hired by Hungarian prince Nikolaus I of the **Esterházy** family.

For over 30 years, Haydn was Director of Court Music for the wealthy Esterházy family, who owned 25 palaces and over a half million acres of land. Haydn was required to wear a uniform, care for instruments, and compose and rehearse all music requested by the Prince. Because ambassadors and royalty often visited the estates, Haydn became well known throughout Europe.

Franz Joseph Haydn (1794)
by William Daniell (1769–1837)

A performance of Haydn's oratorio The Creation (1808), painting by Balthasar Wigand (1771–1846)

Two-page background: The Esterházy Estate (1812) by Albert Christoph Dies (1755–1822)

Haydn's Keyboard Works

Haydn was a close friend of Mozart, and the two composers influenced each other's work. Haydn's optimistic and witty style can be heard in his many symphonies and piano sonatas. His final three piano sonatas were influenced by the virtuoso pianists and rich-sounding Broadwood pianos he heard during visits to London. *Variations in F Minor*, Hob. XVII:6, is considered a keyboard masterpiece, and the *Concerto in D Major*, Hob. XVIII:11, is a popular piano concerto.

Haydn's works are identified by the **Hoboken (Hob.)** catalogue numbers by Anthony van Hoboken (Dutch, 1887–1983).

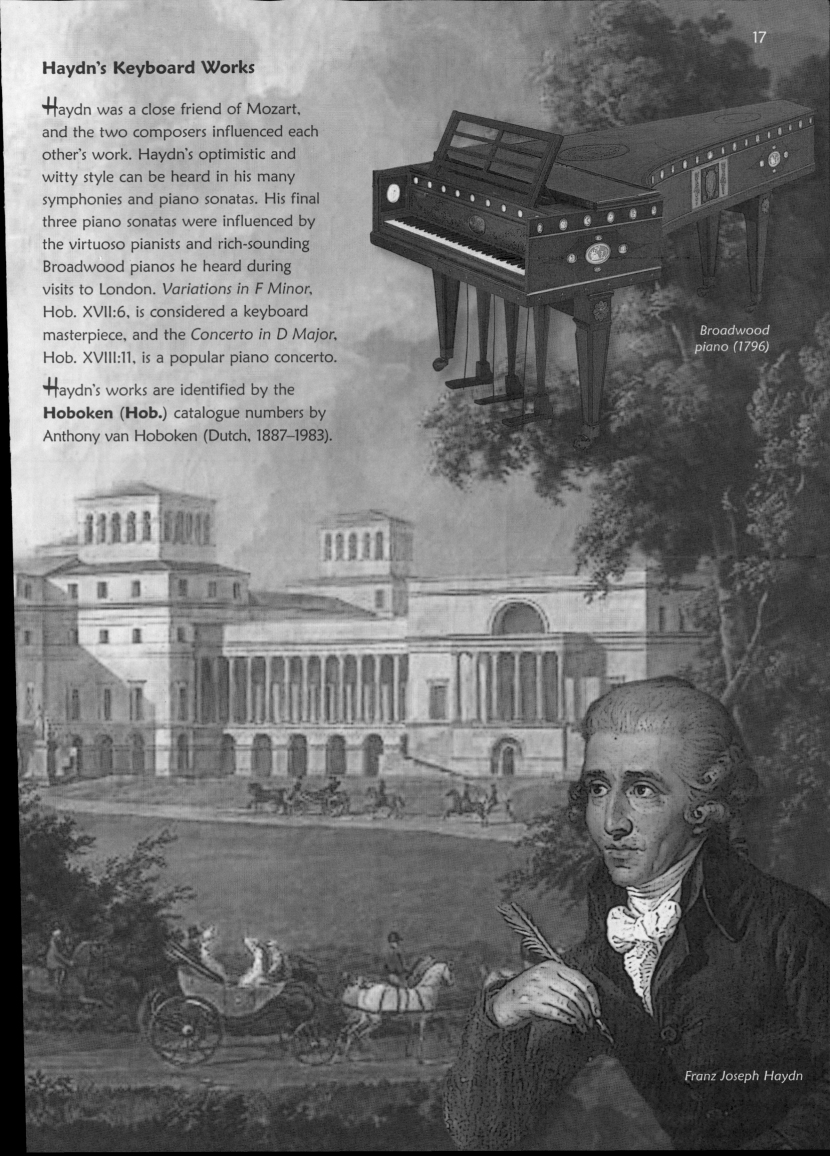

Broadwood piano (1796)

Franz Joseph Haydn

Summary: Classical Keyboard Composers

- Bach's sons *Wilhelm Friedemann, Carl Philipp Emanuel,* and *Johann Christian* composed music that set the stage for the Classical period.

- *Bartolomeo Cristofori* invented the piano, which was the first keyboard instrument capable of a wide range of dynamics.

- *Sonatas, concertos, symphonies,* and *chamber music* were common musical forms during the Classical period.

- *Wolfgang Amadeus Mozart,* one of the most famous child prodigies, wrote numerous keyboard sonatas and piano concertos—many of which were influenced by his love of opera.

- *Franz Joseph Haydn* spent many years working as music director and composer for the royal Esterházy family. His keyboard sonatas display the refinement of Classical style.

Listening Guide

Track 5: 12 Variations on "Ah, vous dirai-je, maman" ("Twinkle, Twinkle, Little Star" Variations), K. 265
by Wolfgang Amadeus Mozart
(Classical-period piano variations)

The variations showcase different keyboard techniques common to the Classical period: decorative scales and arpeggios, hand crossings, and brilliant ornaments.

Track 6: "Allegro con brio"
from Sonata in D Major, Hob. XVI:37
by Franz Joseph Haydn
(Classical-period sonata movement)

This opening movement of one of Haydn's most popular sonatas is cheerful and lighthearted.

Additional Listening: "Hungarian Rondo" (3rd movement) *from Piano Concerto in D Major, Hob. XVIII:11, by Franz Joseph Haydn* • "Rondo Alla Turca" *from Sonata in A Major, K. 331, by Wolfgang Amadeus Mozart* • Solfeggietto *by C. P. E. Bach*

Connect the Dots

Draw lines to connect each term with its matching definition.

chamber music •

Pre-Classical •

cadenzas •

Köchel •

Esterházy •

Hoboken •

Nannerl •

movements •

- *freely played sections in a concerto that show off the skills of the soloist*

- *numbering system for Haydn's works*

- *Wolfgang Amadeus Mozart's sister*

- *royal family who employed Haydn*

- *divisions of large musical compositions*

- *period directly after the death of Johann Sebastian Bach*

- *small instrumental groups with one player on each part*

- *numbering system for Mozart's works*

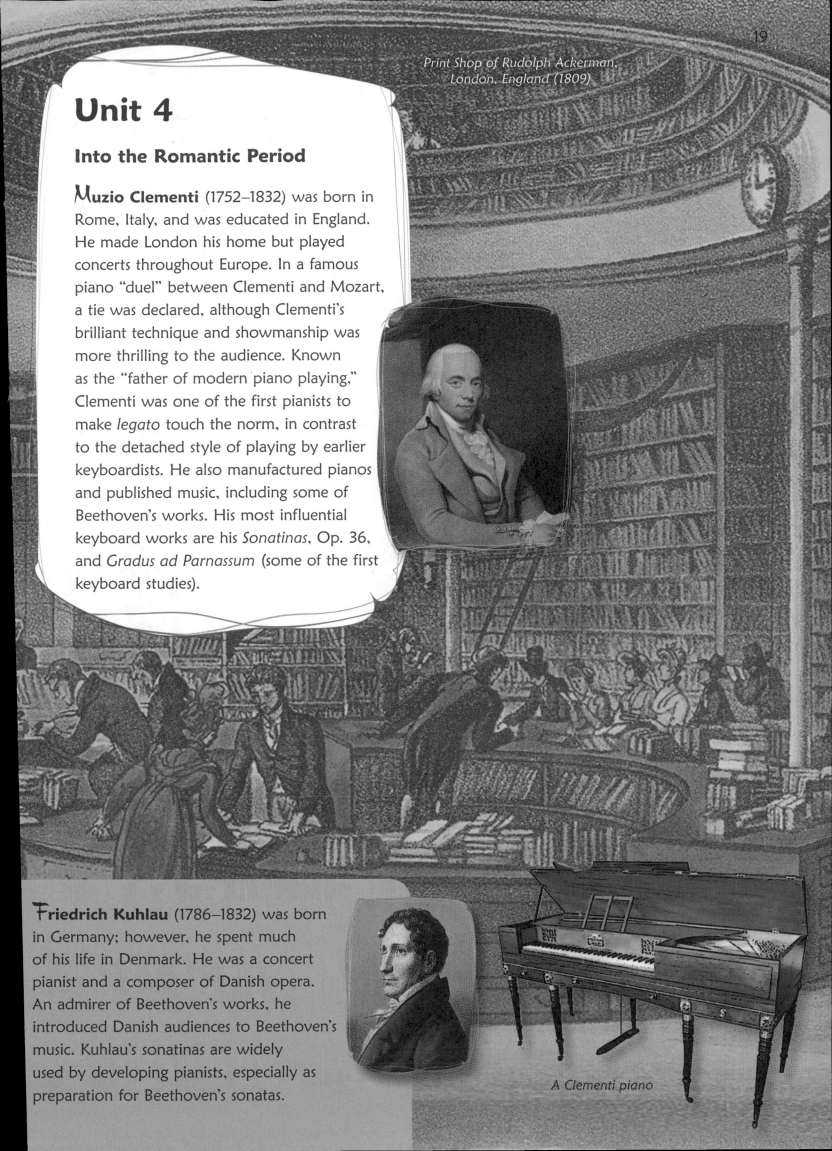

Print Shop of Rudolph Ackerman, London, England (1809)

Unit 4

Into the Romantic Period

Muzio Clementi (1752–1832) was born in Rome, Italy, and was educated in England. He made London his home but played concerts throughout Europe. In a famous piano "duel" between Clementi and Mozart, a tie was declared, although Clementi's brilliant technique and showmanship was more thrilling to the audience. Known as the "father of modern piano playing," Clementi was one of the first pianists to make *legato* touch the norm, in contrast to the detached style of playing by earlier keyboardists. He also manufactured pianos and published music, including some of Beethoven's works. His most influential keyboard works are his *Sonatinas*, Op. 36, and *Gradus ad Parnassum* (some of the first keyboard studies).

Friedrich Kuhlau (1786–1832) was born in Germany; however, he spent much of his life in Denmark. He was a concert pianist and a composer of Danish opera. An admirer of Beethoven's works, he introduced Danish audiences to Beethoven's music. Kuhlau's sonatinas are widely used by developing pianists, especially as preparation for Beethoven's sonatas.

A Clementi piano

Ludwig van Beethoven

As a young man, **Ludwig van Beethoven** (1770–1827) traveled from his birthplace in Bonn, Germany, to Vienna, Austria, to study with Haydn. He spent the rest of his life there. He was a virtuoso pianist, known for powerful improvisations. At the height of his fame, he began to lose his hearing. Total deafness forced him to focus on composition, where he revealed his anguish. He experimented with Classical forms—sonatas, concertos, chamber music, and symphonies—deepening their expression. These works link the Classical and Romantic periods.

The Course of Empire: The Arcadia or Pastoral State (1834) by Thomas Cole (1801–1848)

Beethoven's Pianos

Because of Beethoven's fame, piano manufacturers often gave him pianos. In 1803, he was presented with a French piano by Sébastien Érard (1752–1831) that was sturdier than most Viennese pianos of the time. He praised the "singing" quality of pianos by Johann Streicher (1761–1833). In 1817, the English Broadwood company sent him a six-octave piano that pleased him with its full, rich tone. An 1826 piano by Conrad Graf (1782–1851) had four treble strings. These were added with the hope that the extra sound could be heard by the hearing-impaired composer.

Portrait of Ludwig van Beethoven (1803) by Christian Horneman (1765–1844)

Beethoven's Broadwood piano (1817)

A page from the "Moonlight Sonata"

Portrait of Ludwig van Beethoven *(1806)*
by Isidor Neugass (1780–1847)

*Beethoven at the premiere
of his Symphony No. 9*

*Johann Nepomuk Maelzel (1772–1838)
made Beethoven's hearing devices. He also
patented the metronome. Beethoven first
indicated metronome markings in 1817.*

Beethoven's
"ear trumpets"

*Sketch of Beethoven's studio
by Johann Hoechle (1790–1835)*

Beethoven's Keyboard Works

Beethoven's 32 piano sonatas, written throughout his life, are a landmark in piano literature. They can be divided into three periods—early, middle, and late—that parallel the development of Beethoven's deafness. Many of the sonatas are known by nicknames. Famous from his early period are the "Pathétique" and "Moonlight" sonatas. His middle period, in which he became overwhelmed by his increasing hearing loss, includes the "Tempest," "Appassionata," and "Les Adieux" sonatas. The late sonatas show his withdrawal into a silent, spiritual world.

Two of Beethoven's most famous piano pieces are the rondos "Rage over a Lost Penny" and "Für Elise." The latter was discovered after his death and not published until 1867. Beethoven composed five piano concertos, several for his own public performances. The fifth concerto, known as the "Emperor" concerto, is one of the most frequently performed piano concertos today.

Beethoven's works are identified by **opus** (**Op.**) numbers, a common numbering system in the 19th and early 20th centuries. Opus numbers catalogue a composer's works chronologically and are usually assigned when a piece or group of pieces is published.

The Tree of Crows (1822)
by Caspar David Friedrich
(1774–1840)

Franz Schubert

Living in Vienna his entire life, **Franz Schubert** (Austrian, 1797–1828) never held an important musical position, achieved financial success, or had international fame in his lifetime. Most of his works were performed informally, sometimes in what became known as **Schubertiads**—evenings of poetry readings, party games, dancing, and listening to Schubert's compositions. He died at the age of 31 from typhoid fever.

Schubert at age 17

Der Erlkönig by Moritz von Schwind (1804–1871)

Schubert was a master at composing melodies and was able to capture vivid scenes in his songs. In "Der Erlkönig" (The Earl King), persistent repeated octaves in the piano part suggest a galloping horse and the sound of an Earl King in pursuit of a terrified father and his sick child.

Schubert's Keyboard Works and Songs

Schubert composed many short, freely composed **miniatures**, such as **impromptus** (improvisations) and **moments musicaux** (musical moments). He also wrote more than 600 **art songs** or **lieder** (German poems set to music for piano and voice). Like many Romantic composers, Schubert was inspired by nature and pastoral imagery. He depicted it in many of his songs and song cycles, such as *Winterreise* (Winter Journey), *Schwanengesang* (Swan Song), and *Die Schöne Müllerin* (The Lovely Maid of the Mill).

Schubert's more than 400 dances for solo piano include **waltzes**, **écossaises**, **German dances**, and **ländlers**, probably written for his friends to dance. One of Schubert's most technically demanding piano pieces is the *Wanderer Fantasy*, D. 760, a four-movement work based on a theme from his song "The Wanderer." His many **piano duets** (works written for one piano, four hands) are greatly admired. The *March Militaire*, D. 733, No. 1, is one of his most famous duets, and the *Fantasie in F Minor*, D. 940, is recognized as a masterpiece.

Schubert's works are identified by **Deutsch** (**D.**) catalogue numbers by Otto Erich Deutsch (Austrian, 1883–1967).

Early 19th-Century Composers

At age seven, the talented **Johann Nepomuk Hummel** (Austrian, 1778–1837) studied and lived with Mozart, without charge. Hummel later succeeded Haydn as Court Composer for the Esterházy family. In 1828, Hummel's *Klavierschule (Keyboard School)* sold thousands of copies within days of its publication. It suggested new ways for playing ornaments and for fingering. Hummel's music links late-Classical and early-Romantic styles.

Weber conducting

A virtuoso pianist, **Carl Maria von Weber** (German, 1786–1826) introduced dramatic keyboard techniques in his music—tremolos, wide leaps, arpeggios, and other effects—that influenced later Romantic composers. A brilliant conductor, he was one of the first to stand in front of the orchestra. He is now known primarily as an opera composer.

Hummel

Anton Diabelli (Austrian, 1781–1858) was a composer, music publisher, and piano and guitar teacher. Diabelli & Company, his Viennese publishing house, gained international fame by publishing the music of Schubert. Diabelli's sonatinas, another mark of his legacy, are still taught to young pianists today. However, his name is perhaps best known by the title of Beethoven's *Diabelli Variations*, considered one of the greatest variation sets of all time.

Late 18th-century Vienna

Summary:
Into the Romantic Period

- *Muzio Clementi* and *Friedrich Kuhlau* composed many works that serve as preparatory pieces for Beethoven's masterworks.

- *Ludwig van Beethoven* composed experimental works that used traditional forms of the Classical period but with new, surprising musical ideas.

- *Franz Schubert* composed many vocal and piano miniatures, lieder, dances, and duets.

- Influential early 19th-century composers included *Johann Nepomuk Hummel, Carl Maria von Weber,* and *Anton Diabelli.*

Listening Guide

Track 7: Für Elise
by Ludwig van Beethoven
(rondo)

The well-known opening theme alternates with sections of new material.

Track 8: March Militaire, D. 733
by Franz Schubert
(piano duet)

Schubert composed this when he was teaching Count Esterházy's daughters in Hungary. A lyrical section contrasts with the march.

Additional Listening: Sonata No. 14 in C-Sharp Minor ("Moonlight"), Op. 27, No. 2, *by Ludwig van Beethoven* • Sonatina, Op. 36, No. 1, *by Muzio Clementi* • Sonatina, Op. 55, No. 1, *by Friedrich Kuhlau*

Crossword

Complete the puzzle using the word that matches the definition. Choose from these words:

five	**opus**
Emperor	**Deutsch**
lieder	**impromptu**

Across

1. nickname of Beethoven's last piano concerto

2. numbering system for Beethoven's works

3. numbering system for Schubert's works

Down

1. German poems set to music for piano and voice

2. an improvisation

3. number of Beethoven's piano concertos

Unit 5

Early Romantic Piano Composers

The 19th-century keyboard composers greatly expanded the works for piano. **Piano repertoire** refers to all of the pieces written for the piano. **Standard repertoire** (also known as concert repertoire) includes works that have proven to have lasting musical value and are performed regularly. New works are often added to the standard repertoire, including "rediscovered" works from the past.

During the 19th century, as piano music became more complex, exercises became part of daily routines for aspiring pianists. Leading piano teachers of the time began to compose exercises, **études** (studies), and other pieces written with students or amateur players in mind. Although not usually heard in concerts, many of these studies have artistic value beyond their educational purposes and are heard today in student recitals.

The library at the Paris Conservatory of Music (1895)

Carl Czerny

At age 10, **Carl Czerny** (Austrian, 1791–1857) became a pupil of Beethoven. Czerny composed thousands of études that were used to train pianists to play Beethoven's sonatas and other difficult repertoire. They continue to be widely used today. His most famous studies include *The School of Velocity*, Op. 299, and *The Art of Finger Dexterity*, Op. 740.

Heller

Burgmüller

Gurlitt

Charles-Louis Hanon (French, 1819–1900) wrote a set of 60 exercises, *The Virtuoso Pianist* (1874), that is widely taught and may have been instrumental in developing "the Russian school" of piano playing. Other 19th-century composers who wrote études include **Johann Friedrich Burgmüller** (German, 1806–1874), **Stephen Heller** (Hungarian, 1813–1888), and **Cornelius Gurlitt** (German, 1820–1901).

Hanon

Left: The auditorium at the Paris Conservatory of Music

Frédéric Chopin

Born in Poland, **Frédéric Chopin** (1810–1849) was a child prodigy who began performing in aristocratic homes at age eight. While on tour in 1830, political upheaval in Warsaw made it impossible for him to return home, so he settled permanently in Paris, France. After a successful debut concert there, Chopin soon earned a good living by teaching upper-class ladies and by publishing his compositions. Presenting only a few public concerts in his life, he preferred playing in **salons** (elegant drawing rooms of the French elite). He died of tuberculosis at the age of 39 after years of illness.

Chopin's Keyboard Works

Most of Chopin's more than 200 piano pieces are still performed today. Chopin created a new keyboard style with unusual harmonies that support vocally inspired melodies. His use of pedal created sounds not previously heard on the piano. Each of Chopin's études explores a technical problem. At the same time, their artistic quality has made them part of the standard repertoire. Many of the études have nicknames, such as the "Revolutionary" étude (which has a turbulent left-hand accompaniment, a dramatic melody, and powerful chords inspired by the capture of Warsaw) and the "Butterfly" étude (which contains a right-hard part that seems to flutter across the keyboard).

Page from Chopin's Polonaise, Op. 53

Chopin

Composer and pianist **John Field** (Irish, 1782–1837) influenced Chopin and other Romantic composers. A student of Clementi, Field composed works called **nocturnes** (night pieces), which were short, expressive, and song-like. Chopin, the "poet of the piano," was inspired by Field and composed his own nocturnes, which revealed feelings of sorrow and nostalgia.

Chopin composed many piano pieces in dance forms. These were not intended to accompany actual dancing, but rather to capture the spirit of each dance. Some of Chopin's **waltzes** (a dance in triple meter) portray the elegance of grand ballrooms, while others are more intimate. Some are fleeting, like the popular "Minute" Waltz, while others are more dramatic. Chopin called his waltzes "souvenirs of a ball."

The **polonaises** are majestic in character and are based on Polish folk rhythms. The "Military" and "Heroic" polonaises express Chopin's feelings about Poland's greatness and its political struggles. Chopin's more than 50 **mazurkas** are based on Polish folk dances and contain shifting rhythmic accents. They express a wide range of emotions, from joy to melancholy.

Like Bach, Chopin wrote 24 **preludes** in all major and minor keys. However, each of Chopin's preludes is an independent work, not introductory music to a fugue or companion piece. His other works include **ballades**, **scherzos**, **sonatas**, a **barcarolle**, a **berceuse**, a **Polonaise-Fantasie**, and two piano **concertos**.

Chopin Performing in the Guest Hall of Anton Radizwill *(1887) by Henryk Siemiradzki (1843–1902)*

Background: Early 19th-century Paris

The Modern Piano

Early 19th-century pianists frequently broke strings or hammers during concerts and would keep spare pianos offstage. Technically demanding music and large concert halls required pianos with greater strength and volume. Newly developed iron frames replaced wooden ones and allowed piano makers to add length to the keyboard and increase the tension and strength of the piano's strings. These newer pianos produced a richer tone than older pianos, and the keys moved faster and more reliably.

Felix and Fanny Mendelssohn

Born into a wealthy German family, **Felix Mendelssohn** (1809–1847) and his sister **Fanny** (1805–1847) were gifted composers and virtuoso pianists. As children, they both performed at Sunday concerts in their home for leaders of European society. Sometimes, Felix conducted an orchestra hired to play his works. Felix's other talents included speaking several languages, skillfully painting watercolor landscapes, and editing music. Later, as Conductor of the Gewandhaus Orchestra, he promoted young performers, premiered new works, and conducted the first performance in 100 years of Johann Sebastian Bach's *St. Matthew Passion*. This revived interest in Bach's music, which was not widely known during the Classical period. Mendelssohn also founded and directed the Leipzig Conservatory.

Fanny Mendelssohn had memorized Bach's *Well-Tempered Clavier* by age 13. Despite this remarkable accomplishment and her talents as a performer and composer, her father insisted Fanny's only profession would be as mistress of her home. She was not allowed to tour with her brother or to publish her own works. She did, however, continue to compose throughout her life, writing songs for voice and piano as well as solo piano works.

Mendelssohn's Keyboard Works

Felix Mendelssohn composed 48 piano pieces that he titled *Songs without Words*. These short, melodic pieces were published in sets of six, and publishers gave nicknames to many of them, such as "Venetian Boat Song" and "Spinner's Song." "Rondo Capriccioso" is one of his most often performed piano works. It has a slow, lyrical introduction followed by a lively rondo. Other popular works by Mendelssohn include his *G Minor Piano Concerto* and masterful *Variations Sérieuses*.

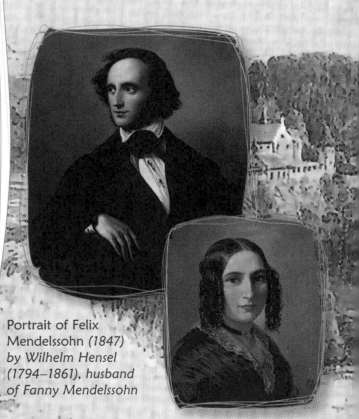

Portrait of Felix Mendelssohn *(1847) by Wilhelm Hensel (1794–1861), husband of Fanny Mendelssohn*

Fanny (Mendelssohn) Hensel (1842) by Moritz Daniel Oppenheim (1800–1882)

Prince Albert performs on the organ for Queen Victoria and Mendelssohn

Background: The Rhine Falls *(1847) by Felix Mendelssohn*

Robert and Clara Schumann

Robert Schumann (German, 1810–1856) planned to become a concert pianist. These dreams were lost, however, when he permanently injured his hand trying to strengthen it. He then decided to focus on music composition and journalism. He hoped his reviews of concerts and his essays about music would raise the musical taste of the public. Like other Romantics, he had a passion for literature, which was often a part of his journal writings and his musical compositions.

Clara Wieck Schumann (German, 1819–1896) was a virtuoso pianist. Trained by her father, she performed in Paris at age 11 and became known as the 19th-century "Queen of the Piano." A friendship between Clara and Robert eventually turned to love, and Robert asked her father for permission for the two of them to be married. Her father refused and would not let them have any contact. After a lengthy court battle, they wed and were happily married. Clara often performed Robert's piano compositions.

Leipzig Concert Hall where Clara made her piano debut

Clara Wieck Schumann

Robert Schumann

An étude by Clara (left) and a burla (a musical entertainment) by Robert (right)

Schumann's Miniature Forms

Schumann excelled in writing **character pieces** (short works that evoke a particular idea, mood, or moment). He created the **piano cycle**, works grouped in sets connected by an idea or theme. *Papillons*, *Carnaval*, and *Phantasiestück* were cycles all influenced by literature. *Album for the Young*, a gift to his oldest daughter on her seventh birthday, contains pieces that capture a vivid character or scene. It includes the popular "Wild Rider" and "First Loss."

Summary:
Early Romantic Piano Composers

- The piano replaced the harpsichord as the preferred keyboard instrument of 19th-century composers. It could be played at home, in small salons, or on a concert stage, and its dynamic range could convey a wide spectrum of emotions.

- During his short life, *Frédéric Chopin* invented a new keyboard style. His unique harmonies support expressive melodies, blended with the damper pedal.

- *Songs without Words* by *Felix Mendelssohn* are among the first lyrical, song-like piano pieces.

- *Robert Schumann* developed the piano cycle, and his wife, *Clara*, was one of the greatest pianists of the 19th century.

Listening Guide

🔊 Track 9: Étude, Op. 10, No. 12 ("Revolutionary") *by Frédéric Chopin (Romantic piano study)*

This dramatic work, which Chopin composed in response to the 1831 Russian attack on Warsaw, has extremely fast and persistent left-hand passagework, as well as a passionate right-hand melody played in octaves.

🔊 Track 10: "Wild Rider" *from* Album for the Young, Op. 68 *by Robert Schumann (Romantic piano miniature)*

This piece imitates the sound of a hobby-horse rider, galloping about a room and knocking over tables and chairs.

Additional Listening: Prelude in A Major, Op. 28, No. 7, *by Frédéric Chopin* • "Spinner's Song," Op. 67, No. 4 *from* Songs without Words *by Felix Mendelssohn* • "Venetian Boat Song," Op. 30, No. 6, *from* Songs without Words *by Felix Mendelssohn*

Multiple Choice

Circle the letter for the correct definition of each term.

1. POLONAISE

    A. a school for musicians

    B. a piece about nature

    C. a majestic Polish character piece

2. WALTZ

    A. a dance piece in triple meter

    B. a Baroque dance

    C. a piece in march style

3. PRELUDE

    A. a type of sonata

    B. an introductory work or independent piece

    C. a sacred piece

4. ÉTUDE

    A. a story from the Romantic period

    B. a study

    C. the house where Chopin lived

5. REPERTOIRE

    A. an introduction

    B. the library where Gurlitt studied

    C. a body of musical works regularly played

6. MAZURKA

    A. a Polish dance with unique rhythms

    B. the name for a music school

    C. a Polish wedding dress

Unit 6

Late Romantic Piano Composers

Johannes Brahms (German, 1833–1897) played piano in cafes at a young age and arranged music to help support his family. When he was 19, he accompanied Hungarian violinist Eduard Reményi (1828–1898) on a concert tour and soon after met Robert and Clara Schumann. Shortly after they met, Robert wrote in his diary that Brahms was a "genius" and published an article praising Brahms's talent and compositions. Brahms and the Schumanns remained close friends for the rest of their lives.

Brahms combined Romantic harmonies and expression with compositional styles of Bach and Beethoven. The three composers are often referred to as "**The Three B's: Bach, Beethoven, and Brahms.**"

Above: Brahms's Piano Quintet, Op. 34

Right: Johannes Brahms (1853) by Jean-Joseph Bonaventure Laurens (1801–1890)

Brahms's Keyboard Works

Brahms's earliest piano works were sonatas, followed by variations on themes by Schumann, Paganini, and Handel—all large-scale, virtuoso compositions. His last piano works, however, are miniature forms that are more soulful and expressive. He titled these late piano pieces **Intermezzos, Capriccios, Rhapsodies, Ballades,** and **Romances.** Brahms also wrote music for piano duet. His *Waltzes* and *Hungarian Dances* for one piano, four hands remain popular today.

Brahms at the Piano (1896) by Willy von Beckerath (1868–1938)

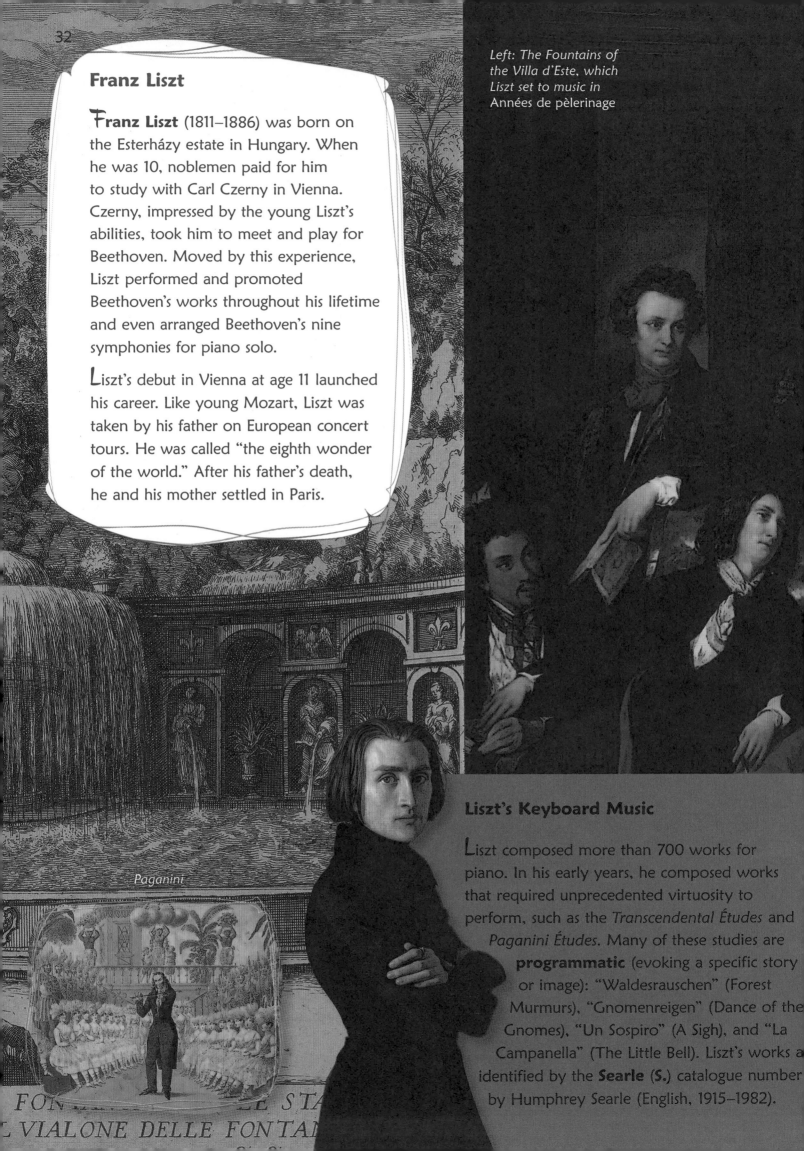

Franz Liszt

Franz Liszt (1811–1886) was born on the Esterházy estate in Hungary. When he was 10, noblemen paid for him to study with Carl Czerny in Vienna. Czerny, impressed by the young Liszt's abilities, took him to meet and play for Beethoven. Moved by this experience, Liszt performed and promoted Beethoven's works throughout his lifetime and even arranged Beethoven's nine symphonies for piano solo.

Liszt's debut in Vienna at age 11 launched his career. Like young Mozart, Liszt was taken by his father on European concert tours. He was called "the eighth wonder of the world." After his father's death, he and his mother settled in Paris.

Left: The Fountains of the Villa d'Este, which Liszt set to music in Années de pèlerinage

Paganini

Liszt's Keyboard Music

Liszt composed more than 700 works for piano. In his early years, he composed works that required unprecedented virtuosity to perform, such as the *Transcendental Études* and *Paganini Études*. Many of these studies are **programmatic** (evoking a specific story or image): "Waldesrauschen" (Forest Murmurs), "Gnomenreigen" (Dance of the Gnomes), "Un Sospiro" (A Sigh), and "La Campanella" (The Little Bell). Liszt's works are identified by the **Searle (S.)** catalogue number by Humphrey Searle (English, 1915–1982).

Inspired by the virtuoso technique of violinist **Niccolò Paganini** (Italian, 1782–1840), Liszt practiced many hours a day and developed a brilliant piano technique. Acclaimed as the greatest virtuoso of his time, Liszt toured as far north as Moscow and east to today's Istanbul.

As the first superstar and international celebrity, his concerts were attended by enthusiastic audiences, including ladies who would scream, weep, or even faint. He played solo piano concerts (without the usual assisting musicians) and called them **recitals**. He was one of the first to perform entire concerts from memory. His vast repertoire included works written by composers from Bach to Chopin, as well as his own dazzling compositions.

At the height of his fame, Liszt stopped performing for fees. He played for charity events, conducted concerts of new music, edited music, and wrote on many topics. Pianists flocked to study with him, and his teaching influenced generations of musicians.

Liszt's popular works for advancing students include *Consolations* and *Valses oubliées* (*Forgotten Waltzes*). *Liebesträume* (*Dreams of Love*) are solo piano arrangements of Liszt's own songs, the third of which is the most popular. The *Hungarian Rhapsodies* have a gypsy flavor. Less demanding technically are many of the pieces in *Années de pèlerinage* (*Years of Pilgrimage*), a set of three suites written throughout Liszt's life that capture the experiences of his travels. Liszt also composed and performed many **transcriptions**—piano arrangements of orchestral, vocal, and instrumental works.

Two-page background: Franz Liszt Fantasizing at the Piano *(1840) by Josef Danhauser (1805–1845)*

The Romantic Era icons are featured: Berlioz, Paganini, and Rossini are standing; a portrait of Lord Byron; George Sand in the chair; and a bust of Beethoven.

Folk-Influenced Composers

In the late 19th century, patriotism was expressed in music through renewed interest in a nation's folk music, dances, and culture.

Returning to Norway after studying music in Germany, **Edvard Grieg** (Norwegian, 1843–1907) decided to develop a Norwegian musical style using Norway's folk songs, dances, and legends. His most popular works are the *Piano Concerto in A Minor*, his *Lyric Pieces* (collections of short character pieces composed throughout his life), and the orchestral suite *Peer Gynt* that contains the famous "In the Hall of the Mountain King."

Antonin Dvořak (Czech, 1841–1904) became an internationally known composer after the publication of his *Slavonic Dances* for piano duet. He used Czech folk elements in his music and also admired and closely studied American folk music. His famous "New World" symphony draws influences from Native American music.

Grieg

Sibelius

Dvořak

Jean Sibelius (Finland, 1865–1957) strengthened feelings of Finnish patriotism with *Finlandia*, an orchestral work that was performed when Finland was ruled by the Russian Czar. Sibelius later arranged it for solo piano. Sibelius's seven symphonies and violin concerto made him a living legend during his lifetime, and he was given a state pension by the government as Finland's leading composer.

Background
Landscape from Finnmark (ca. 1850) b
Peder Balke (1804–188

Above: In the Hall of the Mountain King (1890) *by Theodor Severin Kittelsen (1857–1914)*

Edward MacDowell (American, 1860–1908) was a composer and pianist who used folk themes in his orchestral *Indian Suite*. His piano suites *Woodland Sketches*, *Sea Pieces*, and *New England Idylls* reflect the Romantics' interest in nature. *Woodland Sketches* includes his most popular short piece, "To a Wild Rose."

Russian Nationalism

"The Mighty Five" was a group of Russian composers who promoted a nationalist ideal. They included:

- **Mily Balakirev** (1837–1910)
- **Alexander Borodin** (1833–1887)
- **César Cui** (1835–1918)
- **Modest Mussorgsky** (1839–1881)
- **Nikolai Rimsky-Korsakov** (1844–1908)

Mostly self-taught and employed in other fields, they used Russian folk elements in symphonies and operas, creating unique orchestral colors and a distinctly Russian sound.

Mussorgsky's *Pictures at an Exhibition* is one of the most famous Russian piano works. It is a showpiece for virtuoso pianists and consists of 10 movements, each inspired by a painting.

Balakirev

Balakirev incorporated exotic folk elements into his most famous virtuoso piano piece, "Islamey."

St. Basil's Cathedral (in Moscow) by Nikolay Dubovskoy (1859–1918)

ssorgsky

Peter Ilyich Tchaikovsky (Russian, 1840–1893) was a famous Russian composer of the late 19th century. Resigning his position as a civil servant, he entered the newly founded Saint Petersburg Conservatory for serious music study. By 1866, he was teaching at the Moscow Conservatory. Although he used Russian folk songs, his works are "Russian international"—distinctively Russian, but in the European tradition. His *Piano Concerto No. 1, Op. 23*, is one of the most loved of all piano concertos.

Summary:
Late Romantic Piano Composers

- The large-scale keyboard works of *Johannes Brahms* blend Romantic harmonies with compositional styles of previous periods, while his late works are expressive miniatures.

- Romantic composers were interested in expression and were inspired by nature and literature.

- *Franz Liszt* raised piano technique to an unprecedented level with his playing and compositions.

- *Edvard Grieg, Antonin Dvořak, Jean Sibelius*, and *Edward MacDowell* used folk elements in their works.

- "The Mighty Five" used Russian folk elements, while *Peter Ilyich Tchaikovsky* composed in a more European tradition.

Listening Guide

🔊 Track 11:   Transcendental Étude No. 2 in A Minor, S. 139
by Franz Liszt
(Romantic concert étude)

This is a technically demanding study in alternating hands, with daring leaps in the right hand.

🔊 Track 12:   Wiegenlied (Lullaby), Op. 49, No. 4
by Johannes Brahms
(Romantic character piece)

This is one of Brahms's most famous melodies.

Additional Listening: "The Great Gates of Kiev" *from* Pictures at an Exhibition *by Modest Mussorgsky* • Piano Concerto in A Minor (1st movement), Op. 16, *by Edvard Grieg* • "To a Wild Rose" *from* Ten Woodland Sketches, Op. 51, No. 1, *by Edward MacDowell*

Fill in the Blank

Complete the term for each description by filling in the missing letters.

1. Bach, Beethoven, and Brahms

    T H __   T H __ __ E   B ' __

2. a "Russian Internationalist"

    T __ H __ I __ O V __ __ Y

3. composer of *Pictures at an Exhibition*

    M U __ __ O __ G S __ Y

4. famous Hungarian pianist

    __ R __ N __   L I __ __ T

5. evokes a specific story or image

    P __ O __ R __ M M __ T __ C

6. piano arrangement of an orchestral, vocal, or instrumental work

    T __ A N __ C R I __ T __ O __

7. composed *Woodland Sketches*

    __ A C D __ __ E __ L

Unit 7

French Piano Composers

Camille Saint-Saëns (1835–1921) is best known for *Carnival of the Animals*, a humorous musical suite for two pianos and orchestra. His *Piano Concerto No. 2* and symphonic poem *Dance Macabre* are also popular. Saint-Saëns had international fame during his lifetime and was one of the first composers to promote French music.

Gabriel Fauré (1845–1924) was a student of Saint-Saëns. Fauré served as director of the Paris Conservatory and greatly influenced French music. His works link Romantic style to new trends in the 20th century. Fauré's major piano pieces used many of the same forms as Chopin: nocturnes, barcarolles, impromptus, and waltzes. His *Dolly* suite for piano duet is also frequently performed.

Cécile Chaminade (1857–1944) is best known for her charming character pieces. Her "Scarf Dance" is still taught today. She toured Europe and the United States as a concert pianist, and at the height of her popularity many music clubs promoted her works.

Saint-Saëns

Chaminade

Fauré

The Exposition Universelle (1889) was a world's fair held in Paris, France. The latest in piano technological improvements were introduced there.

"Sudden mania to become pianists created upon hearing Steinway's pianos at the Paris Exposition" (1867) by Charles Amédée de Noé (1818–1879)

Claude Debussy

At the Paris Conservatory, **Claude Debussy** (French, 1862–1918) was not allowed to study composition after failing harmony class. He defiantly wrote outlandish chords that did not follow traditional rules of composition. More progressive professors recognized his genius, and he won the prestigious Prix de Rome arts scholarship when he was 22.

Debussy's music is usually associated with the **Impressionist** movement in art because of its blurred harmonies and atmospheric moods. Debussy knew several Impressionist painters and they influenced him, but he did not like the term applied to his music. After his return from Rome (where he met Franz Liszt and heard him play), he became convinced that a distinct French style of music should be developed.

Debussy

*Manuscript of
Douze Études*

Two-page background: Under the Wave off Kanagawa "The Great Wave" (ca. 1830–1832) by Katsushika Hokusai (1760–1849)

Debussy kept a framed print of this artwork on his wall. His orchestral piece La Mer (The Sea) (1905) is an example of Debussy's ability to create sound pictures. It is also a reflection of his fascination with the ocean.

Debussy's Style

Wanting the piano to appear to have no hammers, Debussy used the entire range of the instrument and created new colors. He also used non-traditional scales and irregular rhythms. Looking back to his French roots, he studied the Baroque composers Couperin and Rameau. He composed in Baroque forms (sarabande, minuet, toccata, and suite) and wrote *Hommage to Rameau*. He proudly signed "musician of France" after his name and, like his predecessors, created music of elegance and charm that would please and entertain through suggestion and delicacy. He was also influenced by Asian art and music, Russian orchestration, and the scales used by the medieval church.

"Debussy's great service to music was to reawaken among all musicians an awareness of harmony and its possibilities. In that, he was just as important as Beethoven, who showed us the meaning of progressive form, or as Bach, who showed us the transcendent significance of counterpoint."

Béla Bartók (1881–1945)

Debussy's
Blüthner
piano

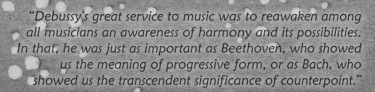

Debussy's Keyboard Works

Debussy's most famous piano work is "Claire de lune" (Moonlight) from *Suite Bergamasque*. This suite includes pieces inspired by Baroque dances, although with more modern harmonies and rhythms. Debussy's *Children's Corner Suite* was inspired by, and dedicated to, his only daughter, Claude-Emma (who he affectionately called "Chou-Chou").

Among his most influential pieces are two books of *Préludes*. These short works display the range of Debussy's compositional style. His late masterpieces *Douze Études* (Twelve Studies) (1915) are some of the most difficult in the piano literature. Debussy described them as "a warning to pianists not to take up the musical profession unless they have remarkable hands." Debussy's music influenced many 20th-century composers.

Debussy's works are identified by the **Lesure (L.)** catalogue numbers by François Lesure (French, 1923–2001).

Maurice Ravel

Born in the Basque region of France near the Spanish border, **Maurice Ravel** (1875–1937) was raised in Paris and became the leading French composer after World War I. Spanish rhythms and style are heard in some of Ravel's music, such as his famous orchestral piece "Boléro." In the years following his training at the Paris Conservatory, Ravel met with other artists and writers known as the **Apaches** (meaning "hooligans" in French). They inspired and supported one another and other controversial artists. In 1928, Ravel toured America. There, he spent time with prominent American composer **George Gershwin** (1898–1937) and visited jazz clubs. The influence of jazz can be heard in Ravel's piano concertos and other works.

Autograph manuscript of Miroirs

Ravel's Piano Works

The piano music of Ravel is carefully crafted, with a balance of emotion and intellect. His 1901 masterpiece, "Jeux d'eau" (Games of Water), opened up a new era of sound that influenced Debussy and other composers.

Ravel wrote many suites with descriptive titles. *Miroirs* (Mirrors) contains five pieces that suggest images as reflected in a mirror, each piece dedicated to a different member of the Apaches. *Valses nobles et sentimentales* (Noble and Sentimental Waltzes) were inspired by Schubert. The *Mother Goose* suite, for piano duet, was inspired by various fairy tales. "Scarbo," the final of three pieces from *Gaspard de la nuit* (Treasurer of the Night), is one of the most difficult works in the piano repertoire. Ravel's works are identified by the **Marnat (M.)** catalogue numbers by Marcel Marnat (French, b. 1933).

Satie

Poulenc

Erik Satie and Francis Poulenc

Erik Satie (French, 1866–1925) composed in a bare-bones style with wit and mockery. His *Gymnopédies* and *Gnossiennes* for piano are known for their beauty and simplicity.

Largely self-taught, **Francis Poulenc** (French, 1899–1963) began formal music lessons after already having successful publications. He wrote beautiful melodies that were light and accessible, and there is a sense of humor in his pieces. Poulenc's *Trois mouvements perpétuels* is one of his most famous piano works.

Les Six

Several Parisian composers met as students at the Paris Conservatory and formed (with the help of Satie) a group known as **Les Six** (pronounced *Lay Seehs*). The six composers included:

- **Georges Auric** (1899–1983)
- **Louis Durey** (1888–1979)
- **Arthur Honegger** (1892–1955)
- **Darius Milhaud** (1892–1974)
- **Germaine Tailleferre** (1892–1983)
- **Francis Poulenc** (1899–1963)

They rejected Romantic and Impressionist styles, preferring to blend "serious" music with jazz, music hall, vaudeville, and commercial music.

Curtain design for Satie's ballet Parade *(1917) by Pablo Picasso (1881–1973)*

Summary: French Piano Composers

- Some French composers of the late 19th century, such as *Camille Saint-Saëns* and *Gabriel Fauré*, wrote in a Romantic style but with more dissonant harmonies.

- *Claude Debussy* composed atmospheric pieces that explore new harmonies and are often associated with *Impressionism*.

- *Maurice Ravel* wrote daringly virtuosic piano works, which sometimes contain Spanish influences as well as elements of jazz.

- *Erik Satie*, *Francis Poulenc*, and other French composers of the early 20th century wrote short, light works often filled with humor.

Listening Guide

🔊 Track 13:   "Berceuse" (Cradle Song)
from Dolly, Op. 56
by Gabriel Fauré
(piano duet)

Fauré gave Dolly, the daughter of a friend, the "Berceuse" on her first birthday. Listen for the gently rocking rhythms of this lullaby.

🔊 Track 14:   "Golliwogg's Cakewalk"
from Children's Corner Suite, L. 113
by Claude Debussy (French piano piece)

This final movement of the suite uses the rhythms of the strutting cakewalk dance. The middle section features a famous love theme and banjo-like effects.

Additional Listening: "Claire de lune" *from* Suite Bergamasque *by Claude Debussy* • Gymnopédie No. 1 *by Erik Satie* • "Pavane of Sleeping Beauty" *from* Mother Goose, M. 60, *(piano duet) by Maurice Ravel*

Complete the Sentence

Write the name of the composer. Choose from these composers:

POULENC   CHAMINADE   RAVEL   DEBUSSY   SATIE   FAURÉ   SAINT-SAËNS

1. _____ composed *Carnival of the Animals*.

2. _____ composed *"Jeux d'eau"* (Games of Water).

3. _____ composed *Gymnopédies* and *Gnossiennes*.

4. _____ studied works by Baroque composers and wrote "Clair de lune."

5. _____ was a woman known for her character pieces.

6. _____ was a member of Les Six and composed *Trois mouvements perpétuels*.

7. _____ was Director of the Paris Conservatory.

Unit 8

Into the 20th Century

Spanish composers **Isaac Albéniz** (1860–1909) and **Enrique Granados** (1867–1916) share many similarities. Both were born in the region of Catalonia, became outstanding pianists, and studied in Paris. Their teacher Felipe Pedrell (Spanish, 1841–1922) collected Spanish folk music and encouraged them to incorporate these folk elements into their compositions. As important Spanish nationalist composers, their most lasting works are for piano: Albéniz's *Iberia* and Granados's *Goyescas*.

Spanish Girl of
Segovia (1912)
by Robert Henri
(1865–1929)

El Jaleo (1882)
by John Singer Sargent
(1856–1925)

Sketches of Albéniz and Granados by Ramon Casas (1866–1932)

Falla

Manuel de Falla (Spanish, 1876–1946) spent seven years in Paris. There he became friends with Debussy and Ravel who influenced his compositional style. After returning to Madrid, he composed his best-known pieces. These include the ballet *El amor brujo (The Bewitched Love)* and the nocturne for piano and orchestra *Nights in the Gardens of Spain*.
El amor brujo includes "Ritual Fire Dance," an exciting piece that Falla also arranged for piano solo.

Béla Bartók and Zoltan Kodály

For years, **Béla Bartók** (Hungarian, 1881–1945) researched folk music in remote areas of Eastern Europe, the Middle East, and Hungary, often accompanied by composer **Zoltan Kodály** (Hungarian, 1882–1967). Together Bartók and Kodály published editions of Hungarian folk songs they had recorded in rural Hungary. Kodály later developed a system of music education used widely in Hungary and throughout the world.

Bartók's immersion into folk music influenced his unique style with unusual rhythms, melodies, harmonies, and scales. His *Out of Doors* suite, "Allegro Barbaro," and *Piano Concerto No. 3* are now part of the standard repertoire. They require brilliant technique and often use the piano as a percussion instrument. His collections *For Children* and *Mikrokosmos* were composed for teaching purposes. The individual pieces range from beginner studies to difficult concert pieces. Bartók's works are identified by opus numbers or the **Szöllösy (Sz.)** catalogue numbers by András Szöllösy (Romanian, 1921–2007).

Bartók

Kodály

Hungarian folk dancers

Bartók recording folk music (1908)

Sergei Rachmaninoff

When **Sergei Rachmaninoff** (Russian, 1873–1943) graduated from the Moscow Conservatory, he received the highest awards in both piano and composition. Soon after, the popularity of his "Prelude in C-Sharp Minor" brought him international fame. After the Russian Revolution of 1917, he left on a concert tour, never to return, and later became a naturalized citizen of the United States.

Rachmaninoff had a threefold career as a composer, conductor, and concert pianist. Considered one of the greatest pianists of the 20th century, he maneuvered the keyboard easily with large hands that could reach the interval of a 12th. His compositional style is an extension of 19th-century Romanticism, with deeply expressive melodies. His two sets of *Preludes* and his piano concertos have never lost their popularity.

Rachmaninoff

Alexander Scriabin (Russian, 1872–1915) was best known in his lifetime for his orchestral works. Today, his 10 piano sonatas and short piano pieces are recognized for their originality and musical value. Virtuoso pianist **Vladimir Horowitz** (Russian, 1903–1989) played for Scriabin at age 11 and also heard him perform. Horowitz championed Scriabin's music and frequently performed his "Vers la flamme" (Toward the Flame) as an encore.

VLADIMIR
HOROWITZ
SOLOIST *with the* PHILHARMONIC ORCHESTRA
CARNEGIE HALL
Thursday Evening, January 12th
Friday Afternoon, January 13th
Sunday Afternoon, January 15th

Concert Hall in the Mansion of Baron Stieglitz,
St. Petersburg, Russia (1869)46 by *Luigi Premazzi (1814–1891)*

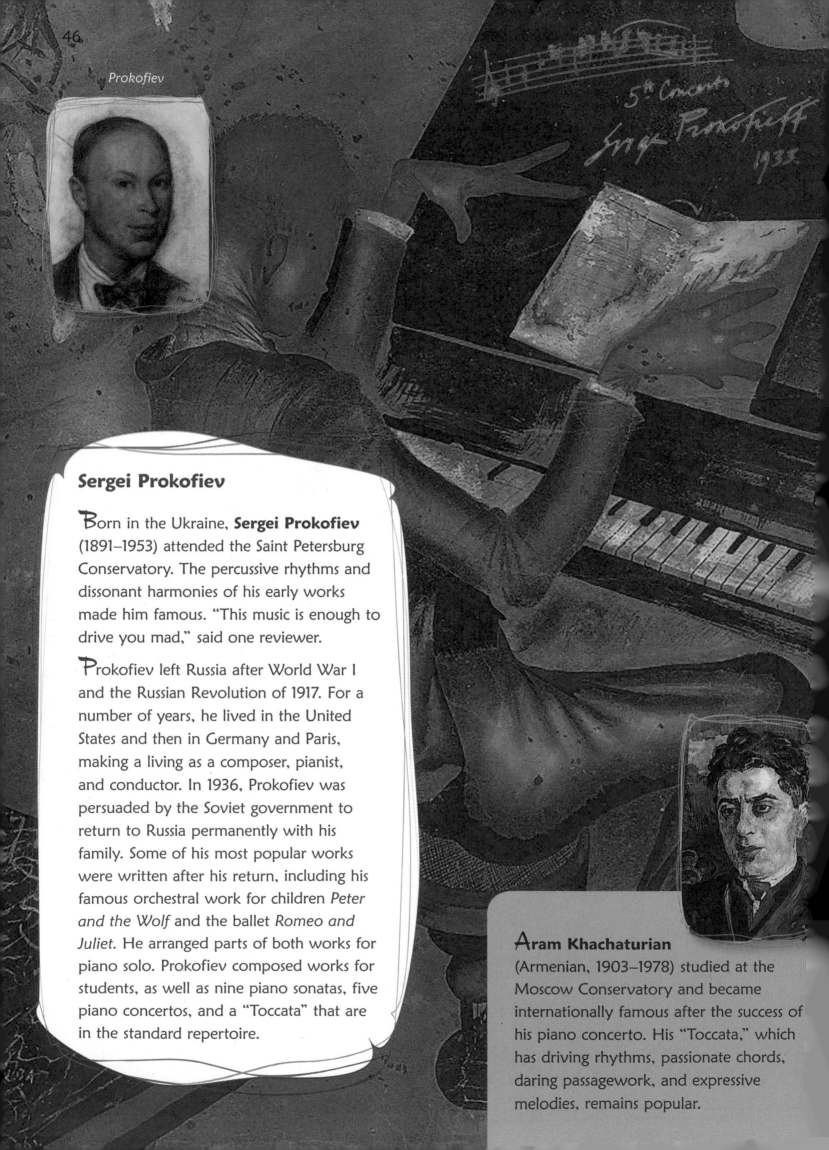

Prokofiev

5th Concerto
Serge Prokofieff
1933

Sergei Prokofiev

Born in the Ukraine, **Sergei Prokofiev** (1891–1953) attended the Saint Petersburg Conservatory. The percussive rhythms and dissonant harmonies of his early works made him famous. "This music is enough to drive you mad," said one reviewer.

Prokofiev left Russia after World War I and the Russian Revolution of 1917. For a number of years, he lived in the United States and then in Germany and Paris, making a living as a composer, pianist, and conductor. In 1936, Prokofiev was persuaded by the Soviet government to return to Russia permanently with his family. Some of his most popular works were written after his return, including his famous orchestral work for children *Peter and the Wolf* and the ballet *Romeo and Juliet*. He arranged parts of both works for piano solo. Prokofiev composed works for students, as well as nine piano sonatas, five piano concertos, and a "Toccata" that are in the standard repertoire.

Aram Khachaturian

(Armenian, 1903–1978) studied at the Moscow Conservatory and became internationally famous after the success of his piano concerto. His "Toccata," which has driving rhythms, passionate chords, daring passagework, and expressive melodies, remains popular.

Dmitri Shostakovich

Under the Soviet regime (1922–1991), Russian composers were expected to produce tuneful music that could be easily understood by everyone. A Cultural Ministry approved or banned music. **Dmitri Shostakovich** (Russian, 1906–1975) spent his life constantly in and out of favor with the government, and his works were sometimes praised and then withdrawn. His *Fifth Symphony (A Soviet Artist's Practical Creative Reply to Just Criticism)* was more conservative than some of his earlier works and put him in good standing again for many years. Shostakovich composed in traditional forms but with "updated" harmonies. He was an excellent pianist, and his two piano concertos are standard repertoire. He also composed a set of *24 Preludes and Fugues* after studying the works of J. S. Bach. Students often perform his *Three Fantastic Dances.*

Shostakovich

In 1948, Shostakovich was forced to admit his music was "in a language incomprehensible to the people" and that he was grateful for the government's criticism.

Dmitry Kabalevsky (Russian, 1904–1987) was a Soviet composer, pianist, and conductor who wrote in tuneful and direct style that was not as harmonically adventurous as his contemporaries. He was influenced by Tchaikovsky, Mussorgsky, and Borodin. Kabalevsky taught children, and his compositions for them are widely used today.

48

Summary: Into the 20th Century

- *Isaac Albéniz, Enrique Granados*, and *Manuel de Falla* were three important Spanish composers who were influenced by Romantic style and Spanish folk elements.

- *Béla Bartók* and *Zoltan Kodály* wrote piano music influenced by folk music of their homeland of Hungary, as well as by their travels to remote areas.

- *Sergei Rachmaninoff* and *Alexander Scriabin* were Russian composers who wrote piano music in late Romantic style.

- *Sergei Prokofiev's* piano music often contains percussive rhythms and dissonant harmonies.

- *Dmitri Shostakovich* was a Russian Soviet composer who wrote in traditional forms.

Listening Guide

🔊 Track 15:   Prelude in C-Sharp Minor, Op. 3, No. 2
by Sergei Rachmaninoff
(Russian virtuoso showpiece)

This prelude begins with three descending loud and dramatic notes that are repeated very softly and accompanied by chords in both hands. An agitated middle section propels the piece to an exciting climax.

🔊 Track 16:   "Joc cu Bâtă"
from Romanian Folk Dances, Sz. 56, No. 1
by Béla Bartók
(Folk-inspired character piece)

The melody of this piece originates from a traditional Romanian "stick dance," which Bartók first heard performed by gypsy violinists. He added colorful, original harmonies.

Additional Listening: "Italian Polka" *by Sergei Rachmaninoff* • Piano Sonata No. 7 (3rd movement, Precipitato), Op. 83, *by Sergei Prokofiev* • Ritual Fire Dance *by Manuel de Falla*

Word Scramble

Unscramble each composer's name to match his nationality:

1. **R O A N D G S A**

(Spanish)

2. **A F H A C N O M R I N F**

(Russian)

3. **T A C I K A H R U H N A**

(Armenian)

4. **T Ó R A B K**

(Hungarian)

5. **O I K F E V R O P**

(Russian)

Unit 9

Music of the Americas

From colonial days, most music in the Americas was imported from Europe. By the late 19th century, European performers toured America, but most American-born musicians composed in the European tradition and traveled to Europe for serious music study. Over time, however, new and unique musical styles began to emerge from the Americas.

Ragtime has a march-like, steady bass with uneven "ragged" rhythms in the treble that originated in America in the late 1800s. **Scott Joplin** (American, ca. 1868–1917) was known as the "King of Ragtime." He played piano in St. Louis saloons, and his "Maple Leaf Rag" was the first piece of sheet music to sell one million copies. Joplin, **James Scott** (American, 1885–1938), and **Joseph Lamb** (American, 1887–1960) were the leading ragtime composers of the early 20th century. Ragtime was important in the evolution of blues and jazz.

Tatum

Joplin

Lamb

Scott

Early Jazz Composers

The word "jazz" (originally spelled *jaz*) was a slang term that meant "to speed things up, making them more exciting." Jazz style became a fusion of West African, European, and American traditions. Although influenced by ragtime, jazz music usually is improvised while ragtime is composed. Jazz pianists developed unique styles as they continually worked to develop greater technical virtuosity.

"Fats" Waller (American, 1904–1943) was often named the top player in jazz-improvisation contests. He was known for his **stride style**, a left-hand accompaniment pattern that leaps between low notes and higher chords. "Ain't Misbehavin'" is one of his hits.

Art Tatum (American, 1909–1956) is recognized as one of the greatest jazz pianists of all time. Nearly blind, he learned to play the piano by listening to player pianos. His playing was greatly admired by both Rachmaninoff and Horowitz.

Player Pianos

A **player piano** (also known as a **pianola**) is a self-playing piano. It automatically plays music that has been recorded onto a perforated (punched) paper roll. Beginning in the late 1800s, the player piano grew in popularity, with sales peaking in 1924. Interest in player pianos declined due to the popularity of radio and phonograph recordings. The stock market crash of 1929 virtually ended its production.

Performances of many pianists and composers have been preserved on piano rolls. **George Gershwin** recorded many of his popular works, including *An American in Paris* and *Rhapsody in Blue*, for the player piano. Many of these recordings have been transcribed and can be performed by pianists today.

Background: Antheil's Ballet Méchanique *piano roll*

George Antheil (American, 1900–1959) was a composer, pianist, and inventor who arrang his most popular piece *Ballet Méchanique* for player piano.

Conlon Nancarrow (1912–1997) was an American-born composer who spent most of his life in Mexico. Nancarrow is best remembered for his 51 *Studies for Player Piano* that incorporated complex rhythms at accelerated tempos. He realized player pianos could play far beyond human capabilities and produce unique sounds. He lived most of his life in isolation and was unknown until the 1980s, when some scores and recordings of his works were released.

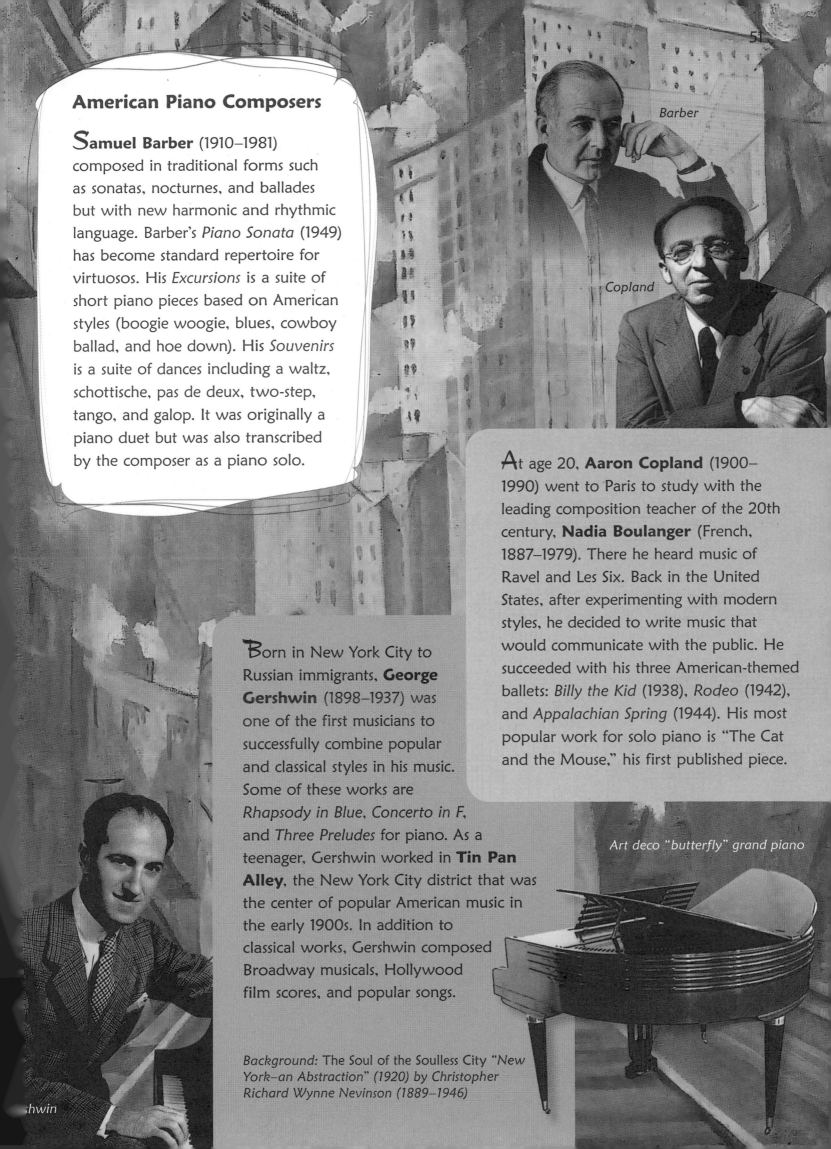

American Piano Composers

Samuel Barber (1910–1981) composed in traditional forms such as sonatas, nocturnes, and ballades but with new harmonic and rhythmic language. Barber's *Piano Sonata* (1949) has become standard repertoire for virtuosos. His *Excursions* is a suite of short piano pieces based on American styles (boogie woogie, blues, cowboy ballad, and hoe down). His *Souvenirs* is a suite of dances including a waltz, schottische, pas de deux, two-step, tango, and galop. It was originally a piano duet but was also transcribed by the composer as a piano solo.

Barber

Copland

At age 20, **Aaron Copland** (1900–1990) went to Paris to study with the leading composition teacher of the 20th century, **Nadia Boulanger** (French, 1887–1979). There he heard music of Ravel and Les Six. Back in the United States, after experimenting with modern styles, he decided to write music that would communicate with the public. He succeeded with his three American-themed ballets: *Billy the Kid* (1938), *Rodeo* (1942), and *Appalachian Spring* (1944). His most popular work for solo piano is "The Cat and the Mouse," his first published piece.

Born in New York City to Russian immigrants, **George Gershwin** (1898–1937) was one of the first musicians to successfully combine popular and classical styles in his music. Some of these works are *Rhapsody in Blue*, *Concerto in F*, and *Three Preludes* for piano. As a teenager, Gershwin worked in **Tin Pan Alley**, the New York City district that was the center of popular American music in the early 1900s. In addition to classical works, Gershwin composed Broadway musicals, Hollywood film scores, and popular songs.

Art deco "butterfly" grand piano

Background: The Soul of the Soulless City *"New York–an Abstraction" (1920) by Christopher Richard Wynne Nevinson (1889–1946)*

...hwin

South American Piano Composers

Alberto Ginastera (Argentinian, 1916–1983) explored new rhythmic and harmonic possibilities within traditional forms, while maintaining expressiveness. He had early success with works based on **gauchos** (South American cowboys), with Argentine folk elements and driving rhythms. In 1945, taking a leave from his teaching post, he visited American music schools and studied with Aaron Copland. His *Danzas Argentinas* (*Argentine Dances*), *Twelve American Preludes*, *Suite de danzas criollas* (*Suite of Creole Dances*), and *Piano Sonata No. 1* are part of the standard repertoire.

Heitor Villa-Lobos (Brazilian, 1887–1959) was the first South American composer to gain international fame. He fused European classical music with Brazilian elements in his many works. "O Polichinelo" from the suite *A prole do bebê* (*The Baby's Toys*) is his best-known work, made famous by pianist **Arthur Rubinstein** (Polish-American, 1887–1982).

Ernesto Nazareth (Brazilian, 1863–1934) was a popular pianist and composer. His music was influenced by African rhythms, Brazilian folk elements, and dances from around the world. His tangos and other piano works combine classical and popular styles.

Argentinian Gauchos (1841)

Villa-Lobos

Ginastera

Contemporary Piano Composers

There is great variety in contemporary piano music. Composers continue to find new ways to express themselves through the piano and to explore the technical possibilities of the instrument. "Winnsboro Cotton Mill Blues" from *North American Ballads* (1979) by **Frederic Rzewski** (zheff-skee) (American, b. 1938) recreates the machine-like noise of a working mill using repetitive tone clusters, some of which are played by the performer's forearm.

Philip Glass (American, b. 1937) describes himself as a composer of music "with repetitive structures," using techniques commonly referred to as **minimalism** (simple harmonies and repeated rhythms that create an almost hypnotic effect). This is heard in his various pieces titled *Metamorphosis* (1989).

Other composers continue to write in traditional styles. *Gargoyles* (1989) by **Lowell Liebermann** (American, b. 1961) is a suite of tone pictures that includes virtuosic keyboard gestures and dissonant, percussive sounds similar to those of Prokofiev. The work uses contemporary rhythms and harmonies to evoke the images of various cathedral gargoyles.

The Future of the Piano

Although the piano is no longer the center of home entertainment, today more people play the piano or keyboard, and hear its music, than at any other time in history. Distinct separation between popular and "serious" art music no longer exists. Musicians trained in traditional music conservatories may become rock stars or composers for films or theater productions. Many performers who play classical concerts also collaborate with folk, pop, and jazz musicians. Musicians use all the resources from the past and present, including acoustic instruments and electronically generated sounds. It appears that the piano will continue to move and excite both performers and listeners for years to come.

Sydney Opera House (1973)
by Jørn Oberg Utzon (1918–2008)

Summary: Music of the Americas

- Ragtime, popular, and jazz music had a significant influence on classical composers and their compositions.

- North American and South American composers combined native folk elements, European classical forms, and dances to create distinctly American styles.

- New compositional techniques, including *minimalism* and complicated approaches to rhythm, give modern composers freedom to create original piano works.

- An appreciation of piano music can be enriched by enjoying the music of today alongside the masterpieces of the past.

Listening Guide

🔊 Track 17:   "Maple Leaf Rag"
by Scott Joplin
(ragtime piece)

The left hand has a steady, march-like rhythm with a rhythmically "ragged" melody against it. The piece has clear sections that are repeated.

🔊 Track 18:   "O Polichinelo"
from A prole do bebê
by Heitor Villa-Lobos
(contemporary showpiece)

This piece depicts Punch, a clown-puppet who carried a stick and had the habit of knocking over anyone who disagreed with him. Groups of white keys rapidly alternate with black keys to give the piece its characteristic sound.

Additional Listening: "The Cat and the Mouse" by *Aaron Copland* • Gargoyles, Op. 29, *by Lowell Liebermann* • Rhapsody in Blue *(recorded by Gershwin on piano rolls)* by *George Gershwin*

Matching

Match each term with its definition by writing the correct letters on the blank lines.

1. ___ George Gershwin
2. ___ ragtime
3. ___ stride style
4. ___ minimalism
5. ___ pianola
6. ___ Alberto Ginastera

A. march-like style of music with uneven "ragged" rhythms

B. player piano

C. successfully combined popular and classical music

D. composed works based on Argentine folk elements and driving rhythms

E. simple harmonies and repeated rhythms that create an almost hypnotic effect

F. a left-hand accompaniment pattern that leaps between low notes and higher chords

Famous Pianists

Alfred Brendel (Austrian, b. 1931) is a leading Beethoven interpreter. He performed complete cycles of the Beethoven sonatas throughout the world and recorded the first complete set of Beethoven's piano music.

Hans von Bülow (German, 1830–1894) was a famous conductor, virtuoso pianist, composer, and editor. A piano student of Liszt, he premiered Liszt's *Sonata in B Minor, S. 178.* Known for interpreting Beethoven's works, he was the first to perform all 32 piano sonatas in a series of concerts.

Ferruccio Busoni (Italian, 1866–1924) was a composer, pianist, conductor, editor, writer, and piano teacher. Busoni's concert transcriptions of works by Johann Sebastian Bach are frequently performed. The *Ferruccio Busoni Piano Competition* has been held every year since 1949 in Bolzano, Italy.

Van Cliburn (American, 1934–2013) won the first *International Tchaikovsky Competition*, held in 1958 in Moscow. He returned home to America to a celebratory parade in New York City, and he was a household name for many years. In 1962, the first *International Van Cliburn Competition* was held in Fort Worth, Texas. Held every four years, it has become one of the most prestigious piano competitions in the world.

Alicia de Larrocha (Spanish, 1923–2009) was one of the leading pianists of the 20th century. Her interpretations of works of Chopin, Ravel, and Mozart are highly praised. She is considered to be the greatest interpreter of Spanish piano music, particularly the works of Granados and Albéniz.

Glenn Gould (Canadian, 1932–1982) became known for his unique interpretations of Bach's keyboard music, especially his recordings of Bach's *Goldberg Variations.* He played concerts throughout the world and then retired suddenly from the stage. He continued to record music of many styles, striving for perfection.

Vladimir Horowitz (Russian, 1903–1989) was a virtuoso pianist who was acclaimed as having the most brilliant technique of all 20th-century pianists and is considered one of the greatest pianists of all time. He left Russia in 1925 and played concerts throughout the world until 1953. His next public concert was 12 years later in a dazzling Carnegie Hall recital. In 1986, he returned to Russia after 60 years for a concert that was broadcast internationally on television.

Wanda Landowska (Polish, 1879–1959) became known for her "authentic" harpsichord interpretations of Bach's works. As the piano became popular around 1800, fewer harpsichords were manufactured or played. Following serious study of the music of Rameau, Couperin, and Bach, Landowska researched European harpsichords and then had new ones built.

Lang Lang (Chinese, b. 1982) is a concert pianist with fame like a rock star. He has performed for heads of state throughout the world and for the opening of the 2008 Olympic Games. With a charismatic personality, he has been influential in making classical piano music appealing to young people.

Arthur Rubinstein (Polish, 1887–1982) was known for his interpretations of Romantic composers, especially Chopin. Like Chopin, he was born in Poland, was recognized as a child prodigy, and lived many years in Paris. He was believed by many to be the greatest Chopin interpreter of all time.

Artur Schnabel (Austrian, 1882–1951) performed all 32 Beethoven sonatas in London in 1927, and made the first complete recording a few years later. Called "the man who invented Beethoven," his performances, editions, and teaching still impact pianists today. Schnabel was also known as an interpreter of Franz Schubert's piano works.

Answer Key

Unit 1 *Page 6:*

1. _B_ portative organ
2. _E_ positive organ
3. _C_ manuals
4. _G_ toccatas
5. _A_ tangent
6. _F_ clavichord
7. _D_ quill

Unit 2 *Page 12:*

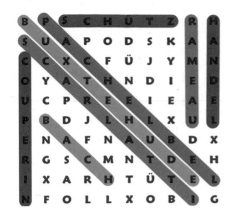

Unit 3 *Page 18:*

chamber music — freely played sections in a concerto that show off the skills of the soloist
Pre-Classical — numbering system for Haydn's works
cadenzas — Wolfgang Amadeus Mozart's sister
Köchel — royal family who employed Haydn
Esterházy — divisions of large musical compositions
Hoboken — period directly after the death of Johann Sebastian Bach
Nannerl — small instrumental groups with one player on each part
movements — numbering system for Mozart's works

Unit 4 *Page 24:*

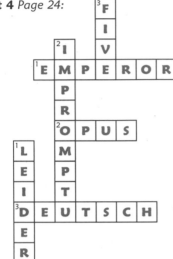

Unit 5 *Page 30:*

1. **POLONAISE**
   A. a school for musicians
   B. a piece about nature
   C. a majestic Polish character piece

2. **WALTZ**
   A. a dance piece in triple meter
   B. a Baroque dance
   C. a piece in march style

3. **PRELUDE**
   A. a type of sonata
   B. an introductory work or independent piece
   C. a sacred piece

4. **ÉTUDE**
   A. a story from the Romantic period
   B. a study
   C. the house where Chopin lived

5. **REPERTOIRE**
   A. an introduction
   B. the library where Gurlitt studied
   C. a body of musical works regularly played

6. **MAZURKA**
   A. a Polish dance with unique rhythms
   B. the name for a music school
   C. a Polish wedding dress

Unit 6 *Page 36:*

1. THE THREE B'S
2. TCHAIKOVSKY
3. MUSSORGSKY
4. FRANZ LISZT
5. PROGRAMMATIC
6. TRANSCRIPTION
7. MACDOWELL

Unit 7 *Page 42:*

1. **SAINT-SAËNS**
2. **RAVEL**
3. **SATIE**
4. **DEBUSSY**
5. **CHAMINADE**
6. **POULENC**
7. **FAURÉ**

Unit 8 *Page 48:*

1. G R A N A D O S
   (Spanish)
2. R A C H M A N I N O F F
   (Russian)
3. K H A C H A T U R I A N
   (Armenian)
4. B A R T Ó K
   (Hungarian)
5. P R O K O F I E V
   (Russian)

Unit 9 *Page 54:*

1. _C_ George Gershwin
2. _A_ ragtime
3. _F_ stride piano
4. _E_ minimalism
5. _B_ pianola
6. _D_ Alberto Ginastera